THE CURLYTOPS
AND
THEIR PLAYMATES

OR
Jolly Times Through the Holidays

HOWARD R. GARIS

[ZHINGOORA BOOKS]

This edition is published by
Zhingoora Books.

Apart from any fair dealing for the purposes of research or private study, or criti-cism or review, this publication may only be reproduced, stored or transmitted, in any form or by any means, with the prior permission in writing of the publishers. All disputes are subject to exclusive jurisdiction of Mandsaur Courts only. For any suggestions and feedback or book on new concept/domain, please contact us at the email given below.

contact@Zhingoora.com

CONTENTS

CHAPTER I

TROUBLE IN TROUBLE

"When do you s'pose it'll come, Teddy?"

"Oh, pretty soon now, I guess. We're all ready for it when it does come," and Ted Martin glanced from where he sat over toward a slanting hill made of several long boards nailed to some tall packing boxes. The boxes were piled high at one end, and on top was a little platform, reached by some steps made of smaller boxes.

"It's a good while coming though, isn't it, Ted?" asked his sister Janet, looking up toward the sky.

"Yes, I wish it would hurry," said the boy, giving his cap a twist, thereby making more of a tangle than ever the curly, golden hair that had given him and Janet the nicknames of "Curlytops."

The two children walked around the wooden structure which they had built, with the help of Tom and Lola Taylor, their playmates, after much hard work in hammering, pounding, and the straightening of crooked nails. Now and then Ted and Janet turned their faces to the gray clouds which floated above them.

"I wish it would hurry!" murmured Janet.

"So do I!" exclaimed Ted.

There was a sudden chorus of shouts and laughter coming from around the corner of the house, and another boy and girl rushed up the path.

"What you looking for, Ted?" asked Tom. "An airship?" for Ted's eyes were again turned toward the clouds.

"Or maybe birds," added Lola, with a laugh. "Are you watching to see some of the birds fly south, because it's soon going to be winter? Are you, Ted?"

"Nope!" as the answer. "I'm looking to see when it's going to snow. Mother said a snowstorm was coming, and I'm watching for the first flakes. What's the good of a toboggan slide when there isn't any snow?"

"That's right," chimed in Tom Taylor. "Now we have this toboggan slide made, we want some snow or else we can't ride down on it."

That is what the wooden structure in the yard of the Curlytops was—a toboggan slide. Tom and Ted, with the help of some other boys and the aid of a few jolly girls, who brought up boards and boxes (though they couldn't drive the nails straight) had, after much hard work, built up a sort of toboggan slide.

Now all that was needed was snow so they could ride down it on their sleds, for none of the children had toboggans—those queer, low, flat sleds, all of wood, with the round curved piece in front.

A pile of big packing boxes fastened together made the high part of the slide. To get to the top of this pile one had to climb on a number of smaller boxes arranged in the form of steps—and crazy, tottering steps they were, but the children didn't mind it. It was all the more fun when they nearly fell down in climbing up.

From the top of the high pile of big boxes there sloped down a hill of boards, nailed in some places and in others fastened together with ropes to make an incline, or hill. This was about twenty feet long, and ended in a little upturn so that a sled would shoot up with a jerk and come down with a bang. More fun!

After several days of hard work the toboggan slide had been finished, and now, as Ted remarked, all they needed was some snow to fall, to cover the incline and make it slippery enough for the sleds to glide down.

But where was the snow? The gray clouds floating high in the air seemed to promise a fall of the white flakes, but though the Curlytops and their playmates, the Taylor children, strained their eyes and made their necks ache looking up, not a feathery crystal did they see.

"Maybe if we whistled it would do some good," said Janet, as all four sat in rather gloomy silence.

"Whistle for what?" asked Ted, throwing a stick for Skyrocket, his dog, to race after, a game that Skyrocket was very glad to play.

"Whistle for snow," went on Janet. "Didn't mother read us a story about some sailors on a desert island whistling for snow?"

Ted and Tom both laughed, much to the surprise of Janet, who seemed a little hurt at their chuckles.

"Well?" she asked. "What's the matter?"

"You don't whistle for *snow*!" shouted Ted. "You whistle for *wind*! Ha! Ha!"

"She's got it twisted!" laughed Tom.

"I don't care!" exclaimed Janet, getting up and walking toward the house. "What's the difference? Wind brings snow, and if you whistle for wind, and it comes and brings snow, it's just the same as whistling for snow."

"I think so, too," agreed Lola. "Smarty!" she exclaimed, thrusting her tongue out at her brother and his chum.

"That's a good one—whistling for *snow*!" laughed Ted, clapping his playmate on the back. "We'll tell the fellows!"

"If you do I'll never speak to you again!" cried Janet. "And if you want to make any more of your old toboggan slides I won't help you. Will we, Lola?"

"Nope, we won't at all! Let's go get our dolls!"

"You'll want to coast down this slide when the snow does come!" taunted Ted. "And then we won't let you; will we, Tom?"

"Nope! And maybe it's going to snow pretty soon," added Tom, with another squint at the sky. It was a very hopeful sort of look, but it did not seem to bring down any of the swirling, white flakes.

The girls walked on toward the house. The boys were beginning to feel rather disappointed. They had worked so hard to get the toboggan slide finished, and now there was no snow so they could use it! Suddenly Tom Taylor gave a cry, causing the girls to turn around and making Ted look up from where he was playing with Skyrocket.

"What's the matter?" asked Lola.

"I've got an idea!" her brother answered.

"Tell us!" begged Ted.

"I know how we can have some toboggan rides without waiting for snow!" exclaimed Tom.

"How? Make believe?" asked Janet. She was very fond of this game of pretending.

"No, not make believe!" answered Tom. "Listen! Have you got any candles in your house, Ted?"

"Candles? I guess we have some. I saw my mother rubbing one on a flatiron the other day when she was ironing a dress for Jan. I don't know why she rubbed the candle on the flatiron, but she did."

"She did it so the iron wouldn't stick to the starched dress," explained Janet. "I should think anybody would know that! Wouldn't you, Lola?" she asked in a rather "snippy" manner and with an upward turn of her little nose.

"Of course!" agreed Lola. "Candles makes irons slippery."

"Well, if you've got some candles we can make our sled runners slippery the same way, and we can toboggan even if there isn't any snow," went on Tom. "I just happened to think I read a story once about some fellows who put candle grease on their sleds and rode down a wooden hill like this when there wasn't any snow. We can do like that! Get the candles, Ted, and I'll go get my sled!"

"Oh, maybe we can have some fun!" cried Janet. "Come on, Lola, let's get our sleds."

"You've got to grease your own runners," Ted warned the girls. "We aren't going to do it for you."

"Oh, I guess we can do it," answered Lola. "Boys aren't so smart!"

Tom and Lola hastened back to their house to get their sleds, which they had not brought over to the newly built toboggan slide, as there seemed no use of doing this until snow came. Janet hastened after her sled, and Ted went in the house to beg some candle ends of his mother.

"What are you going to do with them?" Mrs. Martin wanted to know. "You mustn't play with lighted candles."

Teddy told about the new plan, and his mother said:

"Well, you must be careful. I believe the candles, rubbed on your sled runners, will make them slippery enough to coast down the wooden hill. But be careful. And don't make any noise, for I've just gotten William to sleep."

"Don't let Trouble come out when we're on the toboggan," begged Ted. "He might get hurt." Trouble was the pet name for William Anthony Martin, the youngest member of the Martin family. And he was called "Trouble" because he was in it so often—sometimes through his own fault, and often because of Ted and Janet.

"Yes, I'll keep Trouble in," said Mrs. Martin, with a smile. "And here are your candle ends," she added, giving Ted a handful. "Be careful."

Ted promised and ran out into the yard to meet his playmates. Tom had also found some candle ends, and the boys and girls were soon busy rubbing the paraffine on their sled runners. For the candles mostly sold nowadays are made of paraffine, instead of beeswax or tallow, as old-fashioned candles were made. Paraffine is made from crude oil, as is kerosene and gasolene.

"Now we'll have some nifty fun!" cried Tom, as, having rubbed as much of the candle on his sled runners as the steel would hold, he turned his coaster over right side up.

"We'll have races!" cried Ted.

"But we have to take turns going down," said Janet. "The toboggan slide isn't wide enough for two to go on at a time."

"We can have sorter—now—sorter races to see who can go the farthest," remarked Ted, stumbling over his words in his excitement.

"That'll be fun," agreed Lola. She and Janet were also greasing their sled runners, all the little quarrels forgotten in the jolly good times they were hoping to have.

"All ready now!" cried Tom, picking up his sled. "Who's going to have the first coast?"

"I think Janet or Ted ought to have it, for they started the toboggan and it's in their yard," said Lola.

"That's right!" agreed her brother.

"No, company ought to have the first ride!" decided Janet, who made up her mind she would be as polite as her playmate.

"Jinks!" cried Tom, with a laugh. "Nobody'll ride if we keep on talking like this! Come on, Ted!" he added. "Let's you and me go down together!"

"Oh, don't!" begged Janet. "'Tisn't wide enough, and you might get hurt."

"Oh, we'll not!" insisted Tom. "And it'll be more fun that way. I guess it's wide enough, Ted. Let's try, anyhow."

They found that there was just about room enough on the toboggan slide for their sleds side by side. They climbed up the rickety stairs, made of small boxes nailed one to the other, and soon the two boys stood on the little platform at the top of the wooden slope. They had carried up their sleds with them—the sleds with the candle-greased runners.

"Are you ready?" asked Ted of his playmate.

"All ready," answered Tom. "Let's start!"

They put down their sleds and stretched themselves out on the coasters.

"Wouldn't it be funny if they got stuck half way down?" giggled Lola, who, with Janet, was waiting on the ground below off at one side to see what luck the boys would have.

"Oh, we won't get stuck!" laughed Tom. "Come on now, Ted! Push!"

Together they pushed themselves from the level platform down the wooden hill. The sleds hung on the brink for a moment and then went coasting down as nicely as you please, and quite swiftly.

"Hurray!" cried Ted, as he felt himself gliding along, coasting almost as well as if there had been snow on the wooden toboggan hill. "This is nifty!"

"Great!" added Tom.

The boys were so surprised to find out how well they could coast without snow that they forgot about having a race. As it was, they both came to the end of the slope at the same time. The sleds shot up the little incline and landed on the grass beyond with a bump. Teddy fell off his, but only laughed.

"How is it?" asked Lola.

"Dandy!" cried her brother. "You girls take a ride now!"

Rather timidly at first, Janet and Lola went down the incline one at a time, but they soon grew bolder and liked it as much as did the boys. It really was lots of fun, and as the boards became more slippery when partly covered with flakes of paraffine from the candles the coasting was swifter.

"Now let's have a real race!" cried Ted, after they had been sliding for some time. "I mean let's see who can go farthest from the end of the slide."

They took turns at this, one at a time coasting down the wooden hill and marking where the sleds landed on the grass. Tom and Ted seemed able to make their sleds jump farther than did the girls.

"I beat!" cried Tom, pointing to the mark his sled had made on the grass, after jumping up and away from the little end bump of the slide.

"You did not! My sled went farther!" shouted Ted. "Here, girls, I'll leave it to you!"

The four were trying to decide who had won the race when Janet, glancing back toward the toboggan slide, gave a cry of alarm.

"Look at Trouble!" she exclaimed.

There, on top of the pile of big boxes, having climbed to the platform by means of the rickety steps, stood baby William.

"I s'ide down!" he cried, jumping up and down in delight. "I s'ide!"

"No! No! Don't! Stand still, Trouble! Don't move! I'll come and get you!" shouted Ted.

He started on a run, but he was too late. A moment afterward Trouble was in trouble, for the little fellow toddled toward the back edge of the platform, which had no railing to guard it, and a second later he seemed to topple off backward.

CHAPTER II

THE POSTMAN'S WHISTLE

"Oh, Trouble has fallen! Trouble has fallen!" screamed Jan, as she ran around toward the back of the toboggan.

"Come on, Tom!" yelled Ted. "I guess my little brother's hurt!"

Lola followed the others, and as the four children raced to the aid of baby William a shrill whistle was heard near the front of the house.

"Is that a policeman?" cried Tom to his chum.

"No, it's the postman," answered Ted. "He's taking a letter into our house. Hey, Mr. Brennan!" he called, as he saw the gray-uniformed mail carrier entering the yard. "My little brother's hurt!"

Screams coming from the mouth of William seemed to tell that he was badly frightened, anyhow, and also hurt, very likely.

"Trouble hurt? I'm coming!" cried the postman dropping his bag of mail and running around the side path.

Another moment and the Curlytops and their playmates had reached the rear of the high pile of boxes from which the toboggan slide started. They looked on the ground, expecting to see Trouble huddled there in a crumpled heap.

But he wasn't there. His voice, however, could be heard crying lustily, and it seemed to come from overhead. Yet the little boy was not on the high platform, from which he had been seen to topple backward.

Where was Trouble?

This was the question the Curlytops asked themselves. And it was what their playmates wanted to know, as did the postman.

But before we settle that question I want to answer several inquiries that I feel sure some of my new readers are asking, and among these is this:

"Who are the Curlytops?"

Those who have read the previous books of this series do not need to go over this part I am writing now. They may skip it and get on with the story. Others may wish to know something about Ted, Janet and Trouble.

"Curlytops" was not their right name. As you have noticed, it was Martin. Theodore Baradale Martin was called Ted, or Teddy, and Janet's name was more often shortened to Jan. William was called Trouble as I have mentioned.

The name "Curlytops" was given the two older children because of their curly, golden heads of hair. They lived with their father and mother, Mr. and Mrs. Richard Martin in the city of Cresco, in one of our Eastern states. Mr. Martin kept a store.

The Curlytops were introduced first in the book about Cherry Farm. After that they had fun and adventures on Star Island, they were snowed in, as the book of that name tells, and later they went to Uncle Frank's ranch in the West. At Silver Lake they had fun on the water with Uncle Ben.

The book which was written just before this is called "The Curlytops and their Pets," and tells how the children cared for some dogs, a cat, a monkey, a parrot and an alligator that Uncle Toby left in their charge when he thought he had to go to South America.

Instead of going there Uncle Toby went to Canada. And it was from some of the stories he told of seeing toboggan slides there that the Curlytops had made one in their yard. Then came trouble with Trouble.

"But where is your little brother?" asked the postman of Ted and Janet, as he rushed around behind the high pile of boxes. "You say he fell off the platform, but where is he?"

"I hear him crying!" exclaimed Lola.

"So do I," added her brother. The two Taylor children were among the many playmates of the Curlytops.

"He didn't fall to the ground, that's sure, or else he'd be here now," declared the postman. "There isn't a sign of him. Maybe—"

But Mr. Brennan never finished what he started to say, for just then a little voice, above the heads of the postman and the children, cried out:

"Here I is!"

"Oh, look!" exclaimed Jan.

They all glanced up and saw the head of Trouble thrust out of one of the big packing boxes which Ted and his friends had made into the highest part of the toboggan slide.

The opening of this large packing box was toward the rear of the slide and Trouble was in the box. How he got there could only be guessed, but there he was, tears streaming down his little red face as he looked out.

"I—I wants to tum down!" he sobbed.

At times Trouble talked fairly well and plainly, but when he was excited, as he was now, he said wrong words. Nobody minded that, however.

"Don't jump, Trouble! Don't jump!" shouted the postman. "I'll get you down all right. Is there a ladder anywhere around?" he asked the children.

"There's a stepladder in the shed," answered Ted. "I'll get it."

"I'll help," offered Tom.

Away sped the boys, while Jan and Lola remained with Mr. Brennan looking up at Trouble, who seemed like some little animal in a circus cage.

"How'd you get in there, William?" asked Jan. Whenever the name "William" was used there was always more seriousness than when the youngest Martin child had been called by his pet title.

"I—I falled in!" sobbed Trouble.

"We saw you tumble over backward," remarked Lola. "But how did you get inside the box? Why didn't you fall all the way to the ground?"

"Suffin ketched me and I fell in here," was all Trouble could explain about it.

"I guess part of his clothes caught on a nail, or a piece of wood that was sticking out," said the postman, "and he was swung inside the box. A good thing, too, for it saved him a bad fall. He didn't go far."

This was true enough, for Trouble had swung into an open packing box not far from the top of the platform, so he had really only fallen a few feet—not enough to harm such a fat, chubby little fellow as he was.

"Well, we'll soon have you down," said Mr. Brennan cheerfully. "Don't cry any more, Trouble. Here come Ted and Tom with the ladder. I'll soon get you down!"

As the boys were hastening up with the ladder toward the high part of the toboggan slide, Mrs. Martin came running out of the back door of the house.

"What's the matter? What has happened?" she asked.

"Nothing much, Mrs. Martin," answered the postman, with a laugh. "Trouble is in trouble, and also in a packing box; that's all. I'll soon have him out."

"In a packing box?" William's mother repeated.

"Yes, you can see him," and Mr. Brennan pointed to the head of William thrust out from his "cage."

"Oh, the little tyke!" cried Mrs. Martin. "After he awakened from his nap and went out to play, I told him to keep away from the toboggan slide."

"Well, he went up on it when we weren't looking," explained Janet.

"And he fell off, only he didn't fall far and he swung into the box," added Ted.

"What a narrow escape!" exclaimed Mrs. Martin. "You children will either have to take that slide down or watch William more carefully," she added, as the postman put the ladder in place and began to climb up after Trouble.

"Oh, we don't want to take the slide down!" cried Ted. "We haven't tried it in the snow, yet. It'll be a lot more fun when it snows."

"We won't let Trouble get up on it again," added Janet.

By this time Mr. Brennan had climbed down with the little fellow in his arms. William seemed to be over his fright, for he smiled and asked:

"Can I have a wide?"

"You'd better go in the house with mother," said Ted. "No rides for you!"

"Oh, give him one ride! He's so cute!" begged Lola.

"We'll take care of him," went on Jan.

"Are you all right, darling? Are you hurt?" asked Mrs. Martin, looking William over carefully. "It's a mercy you didn't have some bones broken."

"I guess he would have had if he had fallen all the way," said Mr. Brennan. "But his clothes caught on something and saved him. He just swung into the open box like a piano being slung in a second story window by the moving men. Well, as long as you're all right, Curlytops, I'll be traveling on," he added, as he walked to where he had dropped his bag of mail.

"We're ever so much obliged to you," said Mrs. Martin.

"Oh, yes! Thank you!" called Ted and Janet. They had almost forgotten this in the excitement.

"All right!" laughed the postman, waving his hand to them, as he went out of the gate.

"Now if I leave William with you, will you watch him carefully?" asked Mrs. Martin, as she turned to go in the house.

"Oh, yes, Mother!" promised Ted and Janet in the same breath.

"We'll help!" offered Tom Taylor.

"I'll let him ride down on my sled," said Lola.

"I want to wide all alone!" declared Trouble.

"No, you can't do that!" his mother said.

The postman turned and came into the yard again.

"I forgot to give you this letter," he said, with a laugh. "So much excitement made me nearly forget the mail. There you are, Mrs. Martin," and he handed her a letter.

The children played on the wooden toboggan slide the remainder of the morning, having much fun, and the laughter and shouting of Trouble was as loud as that of the Curlytops and their playmates. Trouble was not exactly a curlytop, for his hair was not like the locks of Ted and Janet.

"I hope it snows to-morrow," said Tom, as he and his sister went home to dinner.

"So do I," added Ted. "It looks like it," he added, with a glance up at the gray clouds.

"If we pack the slide with snow we'll coast lots better," declared Lola.

Ted and Janet, with Trouble, went in the house, having planned to do more "dry" coasting after their meal.

Daddy Martin had come home to lunch from his store, and as the Curlytops entered the dining room they saw their father and mother with serious looks on their faces. Mr. Martin had just been reading a letter, the same letter the postman had left after rescuing Trouble.

"Well," Mr. Martin was saying, "I think we'll both have to take that trip, Mother, and see about this. Yes, we'll both have to go."

"Oh, are you going somewhere?" cried Ted.

"Take us!" begged Janet.

Mrs. Martin shook her head slowly. There was a worried look on her face.

"This isn't to be a pleasure trip," she said. "You children couldn't possibly go. It's about business. Just daddy and I will go, if we have to. But I don't want to go away with winter coming on."

"Why do you have to go?" Janet wanted to know.

"Because, unless we do, daddy may lose a lot of money," said Mrs. Martin gravely. "We wouldn't want that to happen. If we go away we shall have to leave you children behind, and I don't like to do that, however—"

Suddenly the bark of a dog sounded outside, and there came a ring at the front door.

"Somebody's coming!" cried Ted, making a dash for the hall.

CHAPTER III

WHAT SHALL WE DO?

"Here, Teddy! Wait a minute!" called Mr. Martin, but Ted did not wait. He was already at the front door. Trouble had started after his brother, but Janet remained with her mother.

"I wonder who it can be, just at lunch time," said Mrs. Martin. She glanced at the table to see if it were properly set, and began to think rapidly whether there would be enough pie for dessert.

"Will you and daddy really have to go away, Mother?" asked Janet, as the murmur of voices came from the front hall, whither Mr. Martin and Trouble had followed Ted.

"I'm afraid so," was the answer. "Your father had a letter this morning telling of some trouble about business, and unless he wishes to lose a lot of money he and I will have to go and see about some property he owns in a distant state."

"But I don't see why we couldn't go!" said Janet.

"Take you out of school, with the fall term just well started!" exclaimed Mrs. Martin. "No, indeed! You must stay and study; that is, all but William."

"But we don't want to stay here if you and daddy go away!" cried Janet, almost on the verge of tears. "It won't be any fun here alone!"

"No, I suppose not," agreed Mrs. Martin. "And yet your father and I must go. We can't afford to lose this money. I must make some plans. I hardly know what to do. I wonder who came then?"

More talk and laughter sounded in the hall. Teddy came tramping back into the dining room, carrying with him a little jacket belonging to his brother William.

"Look, Mother!" cried Ted. "Skyrocket had dragged this over in Bob Newton's yard. He was playing with Trouble's jacket—I mean our dog was—and Bob saw him and took it away. Bob just brought it back. Look, it's got a hole in it!" and Ted held up the little garment, torn by the teeth of Skyrocket.

"Oh, what a bad dog!" cried Mrs. Martin.

"He didn't mean to!" said Ted quickly. "Bob said he was just shaking it and playing with it."

"I—I—guess he was makin' believe it was a cat," explained Bob, another of the playmates of the Curlytops. "I saw him come runnin' into my yard, shakin' somethin', and first I thought it was a cat. But when I saw what it was—Trouble's coat—I took it away from Skyrocket, and brought it over here."

"We're much obliged to you, Bob," said Mrs. Martin. Mr. Martin, when he found the visitor was not for him, began reading the troublesome letter again.

"Where's Skyrocket?" asked Janet, not seeing the dog with which she and Ted had so much fun.

"Oh, he ran off when I took the jacket away from him," answered Bob.

"I wonder how he got Trouble's jacket," mused Jan.

"I—I took it off when I climbed up on de boxes to slide," explained William.

"That's right!" exclaimed Ted. "I saw it on the ground after Mr. Brennan lifted him down with the stepladder. You brought him out his sweater, Mother."

"Yes, so I did. I thought he had come out with nothing over his waist. Well, I'll have to mend this jacket now. Trouble, why didn't you pick up your jacket after you dropped it?"

"Oh—jest—'cause!" murmured the little fellow, and they all laughed except Mr. Martin. He seemed too worried over the letter even to smile.

"Well, I must get back," said Bob, twisting his cap which he held in his hands. "I—now—I've got to get back."

"Have you had your dinner, Bob?" asked Mrs. Martin.

"Part—part of it," Bob answered. "All but the fancy part."

"Oh, you mean the dessert?" asked the mother of the Curlytops.

"Yes'm, and there wasn't any to-day."

"Suppose you stay and have dessert with us," suggested Mrs. Martin, well knowing how children like to eat away from home.

"Yes'm, I—I could do that," agreed Bob, his face brightening.

"Couldn't he have all dinner with us, and not just dessert?" suggested Ted.

"Of course," his mother replied.

"Maybe Bob has eaten all he can," suggested Mr. Martin, folding the letter and putting it in his pocket.

"Oh, no! I can eat a lot more!" quickly cried Bob. "You ought to see me eat!"

"Well, we'll give you a chance," said Mr. Martin, and they all sat down to the table.

The Curlytop children told Bob about the toboggan slide, which he had not yet seen, as he lived several houses down the street and had had no hand in building up the big pile of empty boxes.

"An' you ought to see me in the box!" cried Trouble, when he had a chance to speak.

"Yes!" exclaimed Jan. "Oh, how he frightened us!"

While the children were thus talking Mr. and Mrs. Martin were conversing in low tones. And once Ted heard his mother ask:

"What shall we do?"

"Something will have to be done," her husband answered. "We must find some one to look after the children while we are away, for we shall certainly have to go. I can't let this slip away from me."

"No, indeed!" agreed his wife, with a sigh. "And yet, with the Christmas holidays coming on, it will be too bad to be away from the children."

"Perhaps we may get back by Christmas," remarked her husband.

Ted did not listen to all this, but he heard words here and there, and Christmas was one of them.

"How long to Christmas?" he asked.

"Quite a while," his mother replied. "It isn't Thanksgiving yet."

"How long before it will snow?" Janet wanted to know.

"That may happen any day now," replied her father, with a glance out of the window. "It was getting colder as I came in. If you children go out to play again you must wrap up warmly."

"We will!" promised Ted. "We're going to play toboggan again," he added. "You can stay and play with us, Bob," he said.

"Thanks! That'll be fun. Oh, you have pie!" he added quickly, as he saw Nora coming in with the dessert. "I like pie!" he frankly admitted.

"So do I," said Ted.

"An' I want two pieces!" declared Trouble.

"Hush, dear," cautioned his mother, in a low voice.

The meal over, the Curlytops prepared to go out in the yard again, to have fun on their paraffine-greased sleds. Bob ran home after his, promising to bring some candle ends, as those Mrs. Martin had found for Ted had nearly all been used.

Such fun as the Curlytops and their playmates had in the yard after dinner! Tom and Lola came back, with some other boys and girls, and they coasted down the toboggan slide one after the other. Trouble was put to bed for his afternoon nap, and so neither Ted nor Jan had to watch him, which gave them more time for fun.

"Say, it's getting real cold!" exclaimed Bob, blowing on his red hands after a coast down the wooden hill. "I guess maybe it will freeze to-night."

"Do you think it will, Tom?" asked Ted of his best chum.

"Well, it's pretty cold," was the answer. "But I don't believe it will freeze ice enough for skating."

"If it only freezes a little ice that would be enough," Ted declared.

"No, it wouldn't!" asserted Tom. "They won't let us skate on the pond lessen the ice is real thick."

"I wasn't thinking of the pond," said Ted. "I have an idea! Come on over here, Tom, and we'll talk about it. I'm sorter—now—tired of coasting on a wooden hill. I'd like some snow."

"Maybe it'll snow and freeze, too," said Tom, as he and Ted walked off by themselves to talk.

That evening, after an afternoon of fun on the toboggan, the Curlytops sat in the living room reading on one side of the table, while Mr. and Mrs. Martin were talking in low voices on the other side. Trouble had been put to bed. It was Friday night. There had been no school that day on account of an educational meeting which all the teachers had to attend, and there was no home work for Ted and Janet to worry about. So they could sit up and read until bedtime.

But, for some reason or other, Ted did not seem very intent on his book. Every now and then he would look up from it and appear to be listening.

"What's the matter?" Janet asked him after one of these periods of listening.

"Oh, nothing," her brother answered.

Janet, too, was not as much interested in her story as she ordinarily was. What her mother had said that afternoon, about having to go away with daddy leaving the children at home, was worrying the little girl more than she liked to admit.

Mr. Martin was just saying something about getting ready to leave in about a week, and Janet was going to ask who would come to keep house and stay with them, when a shrill whistle sounded out in the street.

"There's Tom!" cried Ted, dropping his book and fairly jumping from his chair.

"You aren't going out now!" said Mr. Martin. "It's after eight o'clock, Ted."

"I'm just going out in the back yard a minute," Ted answered. "I promised Tom I'd meet him there."

"All right, but don't go away," his mother said, and Ted promised. Snatching his cap down off the nail, he hurried out, giving a shrill whistle while still in the house in answer to another call from his chum.

"Quiet, Ted! You'll awaken William!" exclaimed Mrs. Martin. "And don't slam the door!"

But this warning came too late. The door was slammed, but Trouble seemed to sleep on. He was tired from his day of play. Janet could hear Tom and Ted talking on the side porch.

"I guess maybe they're going to toboggan a little by moonlight," thought the girl. Then her mind went back to the letter of that afternoon, and she remembered what her father had said about having to go away or else lose a lot of money. Janet did not understand much about business—very little, in fact—but she knew what it meant to lose money. Once she had dropped five cents down a hole, and she never got it back. She always remembered this.

"Who's going to stay with us, Mother?" Janet asked, after a pause.

"Stay with you when, dear?"

"When you and daddy go away."

"Well, we haven't decided that," her father answered. "In fact, it's that which bothers us. We don't know just what to do. If it wasn't that winter is coming we might take you along. But, as it is, we can't."

"We want somebody nice to stay with us," insisted Janet.

"Yes, of course, dear," agreed her mother. "We'll have to write to some of our relatives and see who can come. I don't know just who would be the best, or who could spare the time. And while I know you two Curlytops will be all right, I shall be worried over William."

"Oh, I'll look after Trouble!" promised Jan.

"Yes, I know you'll do your best, dear. And now—"

But Mrs. Martin never finished that sentence. Suddenly, from the yard, came loud shouts, a banging, rattling noise, and Ted's voice could be heard yelling:

"Look out! Look out!"

CHAPTER IV

UNCLE TOBY AGAIN

Daddy and Mother Martin fairly jumped from their chairs and hastened to the back door. Nora Jones, the jolly, good-natured cook, was before them. She had just finished the kitchen work, and was on her way to her room when she heard the shouts of Ted and Tom.

"Oh, Mrs. Martin! Something must have happened!" cried Nora.

"It sounds so," agreed Mrs. Martin.

"Oh, I hope they're not hurt!" murmured Jan.

Just then the shouts of the boys were mingled with laughter.

"It doesn't sound very serious," said Mr. Martin.

The back door was opened and the light from the kitchen shone on the toboggan slide. The light also showed Tom and Ted in a mixed-up mass at the bottom of the slide, each one holding a tin pail.

"WE BOTH WENT DOWN THE SLIDE TOGETHER WITH THE PAILS."

And as Mr. and Mrs. Martin and Janet and Nora hastened out they saw that both boys were dripping wet, and as they untangled their legs from each other and stood up, it could be seen that they were now shivering, for the night was cold.

"What in the world has happened?" asked Mother Martin.

"And what in the world have you been doing?" asked Daddy Martin, rather sternly.

It was very plain to be seen that Ted and Tom had been doing something.

"We—we—now—we were—" began Ted.

"Don't stand here to tell us! Get in the house and into dry clothes!" cried Ted's mother. "You'll catch your deaths of colds out here! Get in the house now and explain later! Are either of you hurt?" she asked, for she noticed that each boy was limping.

"Not much," answered Tom, trying to smile. "We just tumbled down the toboggan slide, that's all, and the water—"

"Never mind now; tell us later," said Mr. Martin.

And when Tom and Ted had taken off their wet clothes, Tom being given an extra suit of Ted's, the two boys, sitting by the fire, told what had happened.

"We wanted some real ice on the toboggan slide," explained Ted. "Rubbing candles on your sled runners is all right, but we wanted some real ice. It didn't snow, so I said, 'let's pour water on our slide and let it freeze to-night, 'cause it's cold.'"

"And did you?" asked his father, trying not to smile.

"Yes, Daddy, we did. But I guess it isn't frozen yet," answered Ted. "We were spilling pails of water down on the slide. We stood on the top platform where Trouble fell off of, and then, all of a sudden, I slipped, and—"

"Yes, and he grabbed hold of me, and then I slipped!" broke in Tom, with a laugh. "And we both went down the slide together with the pails. It was almost as slippery as if there was ice on it," he added.

"Yes, it was slippery all right," chuckled Ted. "And if it freezes to-night we'll have packs of fun to-morrow."

The thought of the fun they might have seemed to make the boys forget their present troubles.

"Well, I'm glad it isn't any worse," said Mrs. Martin. "You boys should be careful on that slide. Just think! You might have been hurt!"

"Oh, you can't get hurt on that slide," declared Ted. "It's nice and smooth. And, anyhow, I didn't mean to slip; I couldn't help it." He laughed as he remembered it, and Jan laughed too. She wished she had been there to see Tom and Ted toppling down the slide together with the empty pails banging. It was this that had made the noise.

"It was like Jack and Jill, falling down the hill," laughed Janet.

"That's right," agreed Tom. "But I guess I'd better be going home," he added. "Do you s'pose my things are dry yet?" he asked Mrs. Martin.

"Oh, mercy, no!" exclaimed the mother of the Curlytops. "They won't be dry until to-morrow. I'll have Nora hang them in the kitchen by the range."

"But I guess maybe—I'd like to, but—er—now—I don't guess my mother would like me to stay here all night," said Tom hesitatingly.

"You don't have to stay here all night," Mrs. Martin said.

"Well, but if my things aren't dry—"

"Oh, wear those of Ted's that you have on," laughed Mrs. Martin. "I didn't know what you meant. That's all right—wear those things of Ted's. He has plenty more. Yours will be dry in the morning."

"And I hope there'll be ice on the toboggan slide in the morning!" exclaimed Ted. "I wish you could stay all night, Tom. Couldn't he, Mother?" he asked wistfully. "We'd be awful good and he could sleep with me and we wouldn't pillow fight or anything. And Tom's better'n I am about spilling things on the tablecloth at breakfast."

"Oh, it wasn't that I was thinking of," said Mrs. Martin. "I was thinking his mother and father would want him home. It's getting late."

"But we don't have to get up early to-morrow. It's Saturday and there's no school!" pleaded Ted, eagerly.

"My mother wouldn't care if I didn't come home, as long as I was over here," said Tom, trying not to appear too eager, for that would have been almost like asking to remain.

"Well, I suppose it would be best for you not to go out in the cold again, after having been wet," said Mrs. Martin. "We could telephone to your mother, Tom."

"All right!" he cried joyfully.

"Hurray!" shouted Ted.

"Be careful! Don't awaken Trouble!" cautioned Mrs. Martin.

Thereupon the boys quieted down, but they were still bubbling over with mirth, talking about the fun they would have sleeping together and the other fun they would have on the toboggan slide the next day.

Mr. Martin telephoned to the Taylor home, explaining about the little accident that had happened to Tom, and suggesting that, if it was all right, he should remain with the Curlytops that night. Mr. Taylor said it would be all right, and thanked Mr. Martin for his kindness.

Janet remained up a little longer, listening to Tom and Ted telling over again just how they had carried pails of water to the top of the wooden slope, spilling down the sloping boards the liquid which swished its way like rapids in a river. And then came the tumble and fall of the boys.

"Boys, as long as you are going to have good times to-morrow I suggest that you go to bed now," said Mrs. Martin, when it was past nine o'clock.

"I want to get a glass of water first," said Ted, going toward the kitchen.

"You can get a drink up in the bathroom," his mother told him.

"I don't want this to drink," Ted explained. "I want to fill a glass full of water and set it out on the steps."

"What for?" Janet wanted to know. "No birds will come to drink at night," she added, for she and her brother had made a bird-feeding station in their yard, and also a little shallow basin where the feathered songsters could bathe and drink.

"This isn't for birds," Ted explained. "I just want to set a glass of water outside and wait to see if it freezes. If it does, then we'll know if there's going to be ice on our toboggan slide in the morning."

"Nonsense!" laughed his mother. "I can't let you stay up until you find out if a glass of water will freeze. It would take too long."

"Not to see if just the top froze over," insisted Ted. "I don't mean until the whole glass freezes solid. I know that would take a long time."

"No, no!" laughed his mother, giving him a friendly little push from the room. "Go to bed! I think it will be cold enough to make at least a skim of ice on your toboggan slide. But not much more. So don't be disappointed if you have to use candles on your sled runners to-morrow."

However, Ted, and Janet, and Tom went to bed filled with joyous hopes for the next day. The boys were almost as good as they promised to be, not having any pillow fight. But they did "cut up" a little, and had to be told, more than once, to get quiet and go to sleep. And finally they did.

In spite of the fact that the morning brought Saturday, with no school, when the children might have slept later had they wished, Tom and Ted were up earlier than usual. Hardly stopping to dress properly, the two boys ran out into the yard and to the toboggan slide.

"Hurray!" cried Tom. "She froze!"

"Oh, what a nifty lot of ice!" exclaimed Ted.

And the sloping boards of the toboggan slide were covered with a film that glistened and sparkled in the sun. The morning air was cold, too, and the boys felt sure the ice that had formed from the water they poured on would not soon melt.

"Come on, Janet!" cried Tom, after breakfast. "Now you can have a real toboggan ride!"

"Me, too!" called Trouble, banging his oatmeal spoon on his plate.

"After a while, dear. You aren't dressed yet," his mother told the little fellow.

Indeed the toboggan was a real hill of ice now, though the frozen covering was thin. And the children had many fine coasts on it, for the sleds went faster than when greased with candles.

Lola Taylor came over, and so did other playmates of the Curlytops, and you can be sure that after this the thin coating of ice on the boards did not last long. It began to wear off and wear thin, first in one place and then in another, the rising sun helping to melt it. And before noon there was no ice left.

However, the boys and girls had had lots of jolly good fun, and Trouble also had his share. As the boards, once they were wet from the melting ice, were too sticky for the candle-greased sleds to coast on, the fun had to be given up just before noon.

But after dinner Tom and Ted found something else that gave them an adventure. A little brook ran through a meadow, not far from the home of the Curlytops, and on a part of this that was in the shadow from a hill there was some ice that was quite thick, and it remained unmelted, as the sun did not shine on it.

"Oh, look!" cried Ted, as the two chums, wandering through the meadow in search of fun, saw the ice. "Look! We can have a slide!"

"Will it hold?" asked Tom.

"Sure! Look at Skyrocket!" answered Ted.

The dog had walked out on the thin ice which held him up. But the boys did not stop to think that Skyrocket was not as heavy as either of them. Also Skyrocket was on four feet, and his weight was more scattered, being distributed over a larger surface than theirs would be. But Tom and Ted never thought of this. Ice that would hold Skyrocket would hold them, they thought.

In another instant they had walked out on it and were just going to run and take a little slide when there was a cracking sound, and, before they knew it, both lads had plunged into the brook at one of the deep parts.

"Oh! Oh!" cried Tom and Ted together, for they were quite frightened.

Skyrocket barked and capered about. He did not know whether this was a game the boys were playing, or whether their cries meant danger. To tell the truth there was not really much danger, as the brook was not up to the knees of the boys at this point.

They remained upright, floundering about and struggling in the cold water amid chunks of thin ice. For the ice was really too thin to hold them.

"Oh, what are we going to do?" cried Tom.

"I'm nearer shore than you are!" panted Ted. "Grab hold of my hand and I'll help you out!"

But as the boys were struggling together they heard a voice shouting at them from the far side of the meadow. They looked and saw a man running toward them. He reached them before they had gotten to the bank where Skyrocket was wildly barking, and, reaching his hands out to them, the man pulled Tom and Ted to safety.

"What in the world are you lads up to?" the man asked.

Something in the voice caused Ted to look up, and he cried.

"Uncle Toby!"

"Yes, Uncle Toby!" admitted the man, with a laugh. "It's a good thing I happened to take the short cut across lots from the railroad. Now tell me why you chaps went in swimming on a day like this?" and he looked first at Ted and then at Tom.

CHAPTER V

OFF TO THE COUNTRY

Skyrocket ran up to Uncle Toby, barking and sniffing around the legs of the jolly man who had pulled the two boys from the ice-cold brook.

"So you remember me, don't you?" chuckled Uncle Toby, as he watched the wagging tail of the dog.

"I do, too!" said Tom. "Have you got all your pets still?"

"Most of 'em!" answered Uncle Toby. "But we mustn't stand here talking, with you boys wet through. Come on to the house. Run! That's the best way to keep from taking a cold! Run!"

"We—we got—all wet—last night, too," Ted informed Uncle Toby, the words being jerked out of him because of the jolting effect of the run.

"Were you in swimming last night?" Uncle Toby wanted to know.

"We were making a toboggan slide like those you told about seeing in Canada," explained Ted.

"And we weren't in swimming now. We were sliding and the ice broke," explained Tom.

"Well, never mind about that now," said Uncle Toby. "Come on—run!" And he ran so fast, half holding up the boys who trotted along on either side of him, with Skyrocket leaping along behind, that by the time the house was reached Ted and Tom each felt quite warm in spite of their icy bath.

"Oh, my goodness! What'll your ma say?" cried Nora, as Uncle Toby rushed the boys into the cozy kitchen.

"Get upstairs and bring them down some dry clothes. Let them undress and dress here by the fire. The water won't hurt the kitchen floor," said Uncle Toby.

In a little while Tom was again attired in his own suit, which was now dry, and Ted had on an extra one of his own, while the wet garments were taken down cellar to be hung near the furnace.

"I guess you boys had better stay in the house the rest of the day," said Mrs. Martin, when she had greeted Uncle Toby and had heard what had happened.

"I have to go home," said Tom. "Thank you for drying my clothes, and I'm sorry I got Ted's wet," he added.

"Well, be careful," cautioned Mrs. Martin, as Ted's playmate left, promising to run all the way so he would not get a chill. But the day was quite warm now, all the ice having been melted from the toboggan slide, and even the water on it drying up.

"Well, what kindly fortune brings you here, Uncle Toby?" asked Mrs. Martin, as soon as she could sit down for a chat.

"Oh, I came to ask a favor," went on the old gentleman, who had traveled in many parts of the world and who had collected quite a few strange pets, some of which he still kept at his home in Pocono. "But you look worried, Ruth," he went on. "Has anything happened? Don't worry about those boys. They won't take cold from a little dipping, even if the weather is getting a bit frosty."

"I wasn't worrying about them," said Mother Martin, with a smile. "But we have had some other troubles. Dick has had word that he is likely to lose a lot of money, and he and I will have to take a trip to see about some property. We'll have to go right away, or within a day or so, and what to do about the children I don't know. We can't very well take them with us. I was just thinking we might get some of our relations to come and stay here while we're gone. Then you drop in. Have you come to tell me that you are coming to pay a visit? I'd leave my Curlytops and William with you and know they were safe."

"And I'd ask nothing better than to look after them," said Uncle Toby, with a smile. "But I didn't come to tell you I was coming here. Instead I came to invite you to my place in the country. I have a large cottage, or camp, as you know, at Crystal Lake, just outside Pocono. I'm going to have a sort of holiday party out there this winter, and I want you and the Curlytops to come and spend some time with me. In fact I'll take some of their playmates, if their folks will spare them. That's what I came for— to invite you all out to my place to have jolly times through the holidays."

"Oh, how lovely!" cried Janet, who heard what was being said.

"Could we have a toboggan slide there?" Ted wanted to know.

"Me tum?" lisped Trouble.

"Sure you'll come!" cried Uncle Toby, catching baby William up in his arms and hugging and kissing him. "There wouldn't be any fun if we left you behind. When can you get ready to come?" he asked Mrs. Martin.

"Why," answered the mother of the Curlytops slowly, "I don't see that Dick and I can come at all. We must take this business trip or daddy will lose a lot of money," she explained to the children. "But your coming at this time is most fortunate, Uncle Toby. As long as you are going to have a party out at your country cabin on Crystal Lake, it will be just the thing for the children. They can go and stay with you while Dick and I are away."

"Of course!" cried Uncle Toby. "Aunt Sallie—you remember her I guess?" he went on—"she'll be there to cook for us and see that the children don't get their feet wet."

"Aunt Sallie," remarked Mrs. Martin. "I don't seem to remember—"

"She's Mrs. Watson, the old lady who went away from my house the time I started for South America, and left you my pets to look after," Uncle Toby explained. "She's a distant relative of mine, and I call her Aunt Sallie, though she isn't really my aunt. But she's come back to keep house for me, and she'll go out to the camp with us. It will be just the place for the older children, and they can go to school there. We've got a good little country school not far from the lake. In fact they can skate to school when the lake gets frozen over, and that will be soon if this weather keeps up."

"Oh, what fun!" cried Ted.

"It will be just the thing for us," said Mrs. Martin. "It will take away all our worries over what we were going to do about the children while we were away."

"And did you say we could have some playmates out there?" asked Janet.

"Yes, bring along some boy or girl chum—one for each of you," replied Uncle Toby.

"I'd like to have Tom!" exclaimed Ted.

"And I'll ask Lola," said Jan.

"All right," agreed Mr. Bardeen. "And they may find some other playmates when they get out there," he added in a low voice.

"Do you mean new pets?" asked Ted, overhearing what Uncle Toby remarked.

"That's a secret," was the smiling answer, and he made a sign to Mrs. Martin that he would explain to her later. As for Ted and Jan they were so excited over the prospect of going to spend the holidays in the country cabin of Uncle Toby that they danced up and down and around the room, swinging Trouble with them.

"I'm going over to tell Tom!" cried Ted.

"And I'll tell Lola," added his sister.

"Wait a while, Curlytops," advised Mrs. Martin. "Let's see what daddy says."

The children felt that they never could wait until their father came home from the store that evening. But he did arrive at last. Ted and Janet were sure he was late, but, as a matter of fact, he was a little ahead of his usual time, Mother Martin having telephoned to him about the visit of Uncle Toby. The latter had come along suddenly, not even writing to say that he was on his way.

"I just got the notion into my head that I wanted the Curlytops and some of their playmates out at my place on a holiday visit," he explained, "and so I packed up and come on. Didn't pack up much either," he said. "Just a bag. And I left that at the station and took the short cut across lots. Good thing I did," he concluded, winking at Teddy.

"You must never again go sliding on the ice until you are sure it will hold you," said Mr. Martin to his son. "Just because it held up Skyrocket doesn't prove that it will hold you. If you don't promise to be careful I can't let you go to Crystal Lake!"

"Oh, we'll be careful!" promised Ted and Janet in one breath.

"I guess this means that you've made up your mind to let them come with me, is that so?" asked Uncle Toby.

"I think it will be the best thing that could happen," answered Daddy Martin. "Ruth and I must go to see about that property. It will take both of us to clear matters up and save my money. I know the children will be in good hands when they are with you and Aunt Sallie. So we'll let them go."

"And can we take Skyrocket?" begged Jan.

"Oh, yes, I guess so," replied Uncle Toby. "My two dogs, Tip and Top, have been sold. I haven't as many pets as I had, though Jack, the monkey, Mr. Nip, the parrot, and Snuff, the cat, I have kept. I want them for company."

"Then if we take our dog it will be just about right," decided Ted. "We'll leave Turnover, our cat, here with Nora."

"Yes, she'll need company," said Mrs. Martin. "And do you really mean it about taking some playmates for Ted and Janet, Uncle Toby?"

"Of course I do! Let Tom and Lola come!"

"I'll go tell them!" offered Ted.

"I'll come, too," added Jan.

Trouble wanted to follow, but as it was dark now, being after supper, his mother decided the best place for him was in bed. And there he was taken, after he had fallen asleep in Uncle Toby's arms.

"But what is this about some other children that are going to be at your cabin?" asked Mrs. Martin, while Ted and Janet were still over at the Taylor home.

"I'm going to take charge of two little Fresh Air children," explained Uncle Toby. "You know I give money to some of the big societies in the city, and these societies send out children to the country in the summer. It isn't usual to send them out in the winter, but this is a special case.

"Their mother, whom I knew when she was a girl, has to go to the hospital for an operation, and she has no one with whom she can leave Harry and Mary. So I agreed to take charge of them this winter, as their mother may have to stay in the hospital a long time to get well and strong."

"Where is their father—dead?" asked Mr. Martin.

"I'm afraid he is," answered Uncle Toby. "And yet it isn't known for sure."

"What do you mean?" asked Mother Martin.

"You see it's this way," Uncle Toby explained. "Their father, Frank Benton, went to the big war. He was heard of for a time and then all trace of him was lost. I suppose he was killed in some battle and never found until after the fighting was over. Anyhow his two children, who are about as old as Ted and Janet, were left with their mother. She took care of them as well as she could until she became ill.

"One of the Fresh Air Society ladies heard about their sad case and she wrote to me. I said I'd keep the children all winter. And now when your Curlytops come out with their friends Tom and Lola they'll find other playmates, and I hope they'll all get along well together."

"I think they will," said Mr. Martin. "It is very kind of you to do this."

"Oh, I like it!" declared Uncle Toby. "I like children and animals. The more the merrier. And now let's plan how soon the children can come back with me."

Ted and Jan returned a little later with word that Tom and Lola could make the trip, and the next few days were busily spent in getting ready. Mr. and Mrs. Martin made arrangements to go on their trip, to try to save the money that Daddy Martin was in danger of losing.

Except for this there would have been no sadness when the time of parting came. But the Curlytops could not help seeing that their father and mother looked rather worried.

"I hope Dad doesn't lose that money," said Ted.

"So do I," echoed his sister, with a sigh.

But they were not sad for long. The day came when the children were to depart for their holiday stay at Uncle Toby's cabin on the shore of Crystal Lake.

"All aboard!" cried the jolly old gentleman, as the automobile drew up in front of the house to take along the Curlytops, Trouble, Tom, Lola, Uncle Toby himself, and Skyrocket. "All aboard!"

"Good-bye! Good-bye!" cried the children, as they piled in. The dog barked his farewells.

"Have a good time!" said Mother Martin, and there was just a tear or two in her eyes as she waved her hands.

"We'll have you all back again after Christmas!" said Daddy Martin.

"Oh, what fun we'll have at Christmas!" shouted Ted.

"All aboard!" called Uncle Toby again, and they were off on the first part of their trip to the country for the holidays.

CHAPTER VI

A FLURRY OF SNOW

Uncle Toby drove the Martin automobile through the streets of Cresco. The car was a large, comfortable, roomy one, all inclosed, so that the cold weather would make no difference. There was even a small heating apparatus, a sort of radiator kept warm by the muffler under the car, so that the children would be cozy and warm even in a snow storm.

"There's Tommie Wilson!" called Ted, as he saw a boy walking along the street. "He's got to go to school!"

"Yes, and there's Bob Newton," added Tom. "I guess they wish they were like us, and didn't have to go to school!"

"Oh, you'll have to go to school as soon as we get out to Crystal Lake," declared Uncle Toby. "Don't imagine, because you are going to have holiday fun, that you won't have to go to school."

"But it'll be more fun going to school out there than it will be here," said Tom.

"Sure it will!" agreed Ted.

Lola and Jan leaned over toward the side window of the auto to wave to Jennie Jackson, a girl they both knew, and Jennie waved back, wonder showing on her face at the appearance of the Curlytops and their playmates going off in an automobile. And when the other children of Cresco learned what had happened to Ted, Jan, Tom, and Lola there were some sighs of disappointment that such good luck had not happened to every boy and girl.

Skyrocket seemed to be enjoying himself very much. He was a well-behaved dog and appeared to enjoy the ride in the automobile. He was perched on the front seat, between Ted and Tom, who sat beside Uncle Toby. In the back were the two girls and the baggage.

"Oh!" exclaimed Ted, when they had ridden on some little distance and Uncle Toby had turned into the broad highway that led to Pocono, several miles away. "Oh, I forgot all about it!"

"Forgot about what?" asked Uncle Toby, as he stopped his big automobile to let a little car shoot out of a side street.

"I forgot to tell the fellows they could use our toboggan slide while we're gone," explained Ted.

"That's right!" agreed Tom. "Bob Newton and some of the other boys could have fun on it after the snow comes. We ought to have told 'em!"

"Shall we have one out at Crystal Lake, Uncle Toby?" asked Ted.

"I reckon we can rig up one," was the answer. "There is a man out there who has a real toboggan, too, one he brought from Canada."

"Oh, that'll be great!" cried Tom.

On went the big car with the Curlytops and their playmates, bearing them to the happy country where they hoped to have much fun over the Christmas holidays that would soon be at hand. The children looked out of the windows of the car. They had made an early start, soon after sunrise, but now the sun had gone under clouds.

"Do you think it will snow?" Ted anxiously asked of Uncle Toby.

"I shouldn't wonder but what it might," was the answer. "Do you want it to?"

"Sure we do!" cried all four children at once, and Trouble added:

"I make a snow man, I will!"

"Well, then I guess it will snow," chuckled Uncle Toby. "And I wouldn't be a bit surprised if we should have a storm before we get to my place," he added.

"Do you mean before we get to Crystal Lake?" asked Janet.

"No, for we aren't going there direct," said Uncle Toby. "We are first going to my place in Pocono, where we'll stay a few days. I have to get some things there, and also take aboard two more children."

"Two more children?" cried Ted and Janet. Then Ted added:

"Who are they?"

"I hope they'll be playmates for you," answered Mr. Bardeen. "I'll tell you about them later. Anyhow, first we'll go to Pocono, and later, in a day or so, out to Crystal Lake. That will give you time to meet the pets again."

"Are you going to take them out to the Lake with you?" asked Tom, who knew about the different animals Uncle Toby was so fond of.

"Well, no, I hardly think so," was the answer. "It will be pretty cold for my alligator, the monkey, and the parrot. Snuff, my cat, will be better off if she stays at my house in Pocono. But you can take Skyrocket out with you."

"That'll be all right," decided Ted. "But it would be a lot of fun if we could have all the pets out at the Lake."

"I'm afraid you'll be so busy having good times out of doors, and going to school, at least a little, that you wouldn't have much chance to play with the pets," chuckled Uncle Toby. "And I wouldn't want any of them to take cold. A dog is all right, romping out in the snow, but frost wasn't meant for monkeys and parrots."

"Where will you get these two new children that are going to be our playmates?" asked Jan.

"They are coming on a train. I expect they'll arrive at Pocono about a week after we get there. I'll tell you about them later. They are poor children, and they haven't had as many good times as you Curlytops have had, so I hope you'll be kind to them."

"Oh, we will!" chorused all four.

"An' I tish 'em, dat's what I do!" declared Trouble.

"Yes, and I'll 'tish' you!" laughed Lola, as she kissed the little chap.

On and on rumbled the big auto, until it came to a small town, which, as soon as they reached the center of it, Ted and Janet remembered.

"We stopped here for dinner when we were going out to your place this summer!" cried Janet to Uncle Toby.

"Yes. And we're going to stop here for lunch again," said Uncle Toby. "That is, if you are hungry," he added with a sly twinkle in his eyes. "Of course if you'd rather not eat—"

"Oh, I want to eat all right!" shouted Tom and Ted and Janet and Lola, all at one time.

"I wants pie!" burst out Trouble, and they all shouted with laughter.

A little later the car drew up in front of a restaurant.

"Why, it's the same one where we ate before!" exclaimed Jan, in wonderment.

"Yes, your father told me you stopped here," said Uncle Toby.

As he was helping the children out of the car a ragged boy, with a pinched and hungry face, stepped up, and, touching his cap, asked:

"Like to have me watch your machine, sir? There's been a lot of autos stolen around here lately. I'll watch it good for a quarter."

"Will you?" asked Uncle Toby, with a kind smile. "And if a thief comes, what would you do? You aren't very big?"

"I'd holler for a cop—I mean a policeman," was the boy's quick answer. "I know the policeman on this beat."

"All right, I guess you can watch the machine," said Mr. Bardeen. "Skyrocket will help you keep guard over it."

"Who's Skyrocket?"

"This dog," and Uncle Toby pointed. Skyrocket had been holding back, for he did not like strangers, especially ragged ones, and this boy was rather ragged. But when Uncle Toby made it plain that the boy was to be regarded as a friend, the dog wagged his tail in welcome and curled up on the front seat.

"What are you going to do with the quarter I'm to give you for watching the car?" asked Uncle Toby.

"I'm going to get something to eat with part of it," was the answer. "I'm hungry. The rest I'm going to turn in to my mother. She needs it."

"Hum," said Uncle Toby, thoughtfully. "That's stretching a quarter rather too much, I think. Now you sit out here in the car, and I'll have the waiter bring you something to eat on a tray. Oh, don't worry!" Mr. Bardeen hastened to say, with a smile. "It won't come out of your quarter. I'll put it on my bill. And I'm going to have a bone sent out for Skyrocket. He'll keep you company."

"Yes, sir. I like dogs," said the boy, with a smile. "I'm much obliged to you. I'll watch your car good."

"Yes. I think you will. Well, children, run in and get started on your lunch. I don't want to get to Pocono after dark, and it looks as if we might get caught in a snow storm, but it may hold off."

The Curlytops and their playmates were ushered to their seats by a waiter who smiled at them.

"Do you remember us?" asked Ted, while Uncle Toby was giving orders to another waiter about sending something to eat out to the boy, and also a bone for Skyrocket.

"Of course I remember you," the waiter answered, as he pushed the chairs under Janet and Lola. "And I haven't forgotten what that little chap did," and he pointed to William, who was staring about the room as if trying to remember where he had seen it before.

"What did Trouble do?" asked Lola.

"He turned the faucet of the water-cooler and let the ice water run all over the floor," explained Janet with a laugh. "Mother's feet were in the puddle of water before we knew what had happened."

"Oh, Trouble!" chided Lola. "Did you do that?"

"Well—well, I didn't do it on pur—now—on purspuss!" stammered Trouble, as they all laughed.

Uncle Toby came and sat down at the table with the children, and the waiter who remembered the Curlytop party from their other visit was soon busy serving them. A good meal on a tray was taken out to the boy in the automobile and a juicy bone was sent to Skyrocket.

"This is jolly good fun!" declared Tom, who had not traveled about as much as had the Curlytops.

"Wait until we get out to Crystal Lake!" exclaimed Ted. "Then we'll have more fun. I hope school won't be very hard," he added in a whisper to his playmate.

"Oh, teachers aren't very strict around the holidays," answered Tom.

The meal was almost over when Lola, glancing out of the window, uttered an exclamation and cried:

"It's snowing!"

Surely enough, a flurry of the white crystals was falling.

Uncle Toby looked a bit anxious.

"I don't want to hurry you children," he said. "But as soon as you have finished we'd better be on our way. We don't want to be stuck in the snow."

And as they went out to get in the automobile again the air was thick with the white flakes.

CHAPTER VII

IN THE STORM

Seeing the Curlytops and their playmates coming from the restaurant with Uncle Toby, the boy who had been watching the automobile got out, followed by Skyrocket.

"Well, I see you didn't let any one take the car," said Uncle Toby with a smile, as he paid the boy, giving him more money than the lad had asked for.

"Oh, no! They couldn't take this car while I was in it," was the reply. "Though I guess your dog would make a fuss, too, if anybody tried it. Two or three men just sort of stepped up to look at the car, and Firecracker growled."

"Firecracker?" exclaimed Ted, with a laugh.

"Yes. Isn't that the name you called your dog?" asked the boy.

"No; it's Skyrocket," answered Jan.

"Well, I knew it had something to do with fireworks," laughed the ragged lad.

"But this is too much money," he said to Uncle Toby.

"That's all right, I guess you've earned it," was the reply. "Sitting in a car doing nothing isn't much fun."

The snow flakes kept on sifting down, swirling faster and faster as the automobile started off, the children calling their good-byes to the boy who had watched the car. They had left him much better off than when they first met him, for he had had a good meal and earned some money.

"Sit tight now, everybody!" ordered Uncle Toby, as they left the busier part of the village where they had stopped for a meal, and drew near the open country. "Sit tight, for I'm going to drive faster, and I don't want you falling off the seats."

"What you goin' to drive fast for?" Trouble wanted to know. "Is you goin' to have a race, Uncle Toby?"

"A sort of race, yes, Trouble," was the answer. "I'm going to race and see if we can get home ahead of the big storm that I'm afraid is coming down on us."

"Do you think it will be a very big storm?" asked Ted, and he looked with laughing eyes at Tom.

"I shouldn't wonder," was the answer. "And, though we have a strong car here, we don't want to get stuck in a snow drift and have to stay all night."

"I should think that would be lots of fun," said Tom.

"What? With nothing to eat except a few chocolate cakes Jan and Lola have in a bag?" exclaimed Uncle Toby. "That is if they have any of the cakes left."

"Oh, yes, we have them," Jan hastened to say, for she and her girl chum had bought some just before reaching the restaurant, and had not eaten them.

"Well, that's all we'd have in the way of 'rations,' as the soldiers call them, if we got stuck in the storm," declared Uncle Toby.

"Then we don't want to get stuck," decided Ted, and Tom agreed with him. The boys were fond of eating. Most boys are, I believe.

What Uncle Toby said and feared about the storm seemed to be coming true. Of course the automobile was very far from being caught in any drift, for the snow had not yet begun to pile up very much. But the flakes were coming down thicker and faster, and the wind was beginning to blow. It did not blow inside the cozy car, which was warm and comfortable, so that the boys and girls could unbutton their wraps. But they could hear the wind swishing around outside, and they could see the flakes of snow dashed against the glass windows.

After riding about an hour, the party was out in a country district where the houses were few and far apart. It was rather lonesome, for they went many miles without meeting another automobile. The snow was deeper here, and, more than once, the wheels of the Martin car ran through little piles of white crystals.

"They've had a storm here before this one that's blowing now," said Uncle Toby, as he looked at what were really quite high drifts on some parts of the road. "It may be worse farther on."

"Shall we get stuck?" Ted wanted to know.

"There's no telling," answered Uncle Toby.

Ted and Tom did not want to say they were glad of it, but they were real boys and they felt that they would not a bit mind being caught in a big drift so they would have to dig their way out. They forgot, for the time, about having nothing to eat.

Passing through a small village, which was now thickly covered with snow from the storm that was getting worse and worse all the while, Uncle Toby drove the car once more out in the country. Suddenly he leaned forward and shifted the gear lever.

"What's the matter?" asked Ted.

"I'm going into second speed," was the answer, and the boys knew what this meant. "There's quite a hill ahead of us," Uncle Toby went on. "Though I could take it on high if it wasn't for the snow, I can't do it now. We'll try it on second, and if that won't bring us up we'll have to go back into first speed."

"Shall we get to your house to-night?" asked Jan.

"Oh, yes," answered Uncle Toby. "Don't worry!"

But Jan could not help feeling a bit anxious. She was more worried over what might happen to Trouble than herself, her other brother or her playmates, for they were all older. But Trouble was used to his mother at night.

How he would behave now, away from home for the first time, remained to be seen. Jan wondered what her father and mother were doing now, and she hoped Daddy Martin would not lose that money. She wondered if they would be poor. That wouldn't be at all pleasant, she thought.

However, her ideas and those of the others were suddenly switched into new places, for the big car gave a lurch to one side and came to a stop with a jolt, awakening Trouble.

"What's matter?" he asked sleepily.

"I am afraid we are stuck," said Uncle Toby.

"There's a big drift right in front of us," announced Ted.

"Yes," agreed Mr. Bardeen. "I thought I could go through it but it's deeper than I had any idea of. No you don't!" he quickly cried as the automobile seemed about to slip backward. He put on both brakes and brought the car to a stop.

"Oh, is anything going to happen?" asked Lola.

"No! No!" laughed Uncle Toby. "Don't be afraid. I didn't change into first speed quickly enough and stalled, or stopped my engine. I'll start up again in a minute. But I guess I'd better put some stones under the wheels, to block them so they won't slide downhill as I start up again with the brakes off."

"We'll get some stones!" cried Ted. "I know how to do that! I often do it for dad on a hill. Come on, Tom!"

The two boys scrambled from the car out into the storm. As the door was opened in came a swirl of white flakes, and Trouble tried to catch them by sticking out his red tongue.

"I guess you'll have hard work to find any stones," said Uncle Toby, looking at Tom and Ted floundering around in the snow. "But it won't be safe to take the brakes off until we get something to block the wheels."

The reason for that was this. The car was now held from sliding backward downhill because Uncle Toby had put on the brakes. But to start up again, even in first or lowest speed, he would have to take off the brakes, and the car might begin to slide down before the engine could begin pulling it up. With stones blocked behind the rear wheels, this would not happen.

"Oh, we'll find some stones!" cried Tom, kicking about in the snow, moving his feet from side to side. Soon he felt something big and hard. Reaching down with his hands, he began clearing away the snow and discovered a stone. But it was frozen fast to the ground, and Tom could not move it.

"I'll help you!" offered Ted, running over to his chum. Ted had not yet found any stone.

As the boys kicked away at the stone, hoping to loosen it, Trouble called out through the crack of the door:

"Is you playin' feetball?"

"It does look like it, doesn't it?" laughed Ted, and then, with a last hard kick, he loosened the stone that Tom had found.

"Good boys!" cried Uncle Toby. "Put it back of the wheels and look for another." He had to stay in the car lest the brakes might slip and let it back down the hill.

Tom and Ted put this one stone behind the left wheel, and then began kicking about in the snow to find another. This time Ted had the luck, finding a larger stone than the one uncovered by his chum.

With hard kicks the two small chaps worked away at the frozen stone. More than once they missed their aim, and they kicked up clouds of snow, making Lola and Janet laugh, Trouble joining in. But at last the second stone was loosened and placed behind the other wheel.

"Now I can take off the brakes and start up the hill," said Uncle Toby. "Hop in, boys!"

Standing on the running board Ted and Tom knocked the snow from their shoes and took their places inside the warm car. They were breathing hard from their labors, and their cheeks were red with the cold, while their coats and caps were covered with snow-flakes.

The engine had not stopped running, though it was out of gear. But now Uncle Toby took off the brakes and began to go into first speed, and slowly the car moved up the hill. The snow was very slippery and more than once the hind wheels spun around uselessly.

"I'll put chains on when we get to the top of the hill," said Uncle Toby. "I ought to have done it before."

Slowly the car went up through the storm, the children almost holding their breaths, as if that would help. But finally the summit of the hill was reached and the danger was over for the present.

"Now we can speed up, after I put on the chains," said Uncle Toby, bringing the car to a stop beneath some overhanging evergreen trees that grew on one side of the road. "Ch'is'mus twees," Trouble called them.

But as Mr. Bardeen was getting out Ted uttered a cry of alarm.

"Where's Skyrocket?" he asked.

Then, for the first time, every one noticed that the dog was not in the car.

Where was Skyrocket?

CHAPTER VIII

A STALLED TRAIN

For a few moments the children could scarcely believe that Skyrocket was not in the automobile with them. Janet and Lola had been so busy watching the boys kick loose the stones, and Ted and Tom had been so occupied in this work, that none of them had paid much attention to the dog. Uncle Toby had also watched the boys, and as for Trouble, catching an occasional snow-flake on his tongue gave him so much to do that he did not look after Skyrocket.

"But where is our dog?" asked Ted, when it became certain that the pet was not in the car.

"Maybe he's under the seat asleep," suggested Lola.

They looked, but Skyrocket was not there.

"He must have jumped out when the door was open," said Tom.

"I'll go back and look for him," offered Ted. He made a move to leave the car, but Uncle Toby stopped him.

"If any one goes back after that dog, I'm going!" said the old sailor, for that is what Uncle Toby had once been. "The snow is too deep for your legs," he added, looking at Ted's short ones. "And you two lads have already done work enough in getting the stones to block the wheels. You know how fond I am of pets, so I'll go back and get Skyrocket. I suppose he's looking for us all this while."

"You'll be sure to get him, won't you, Uncle Toby?" asked Jan.

"Of course I will; unless he's gone full speed ahead back home, and I don't believe he has. Now you children stay here in this car until I come back. And don't go outside. It's snowing harder and it is getting colder. So stay inside."

The Curlytops and their playmates promised to do this, and then Uncle Toby stepped out into the storm. He turned up his coat collar and tramped off through the drifts, which were, each moment, getting deeper and deeper. So fast was the snow coming down now that he could hardly see the marks left by the wheels where he had driven up the hill.

The children looked out through the back window in the automobile and watched Uncle Toby. He was soon out of sight below the top of the hill, and all that Ted and the others could see was the cloud of swirling flakes of white.

"I—I hope he finds Skyrocket," faltered Janet.

"I hope so, too," added Ted.

"He sure is a good dog!" declared Tom.

Then all the Curlytops could do was to wait for Uncle Toby to come back.

Meanwhile the old sailor was trudging back through the storm, going down the hill up which he had lately driven the big car.

"It's easy now," thought Uncle Toby to himself, "but it won't be so easy going back. I'll have the wind in my face and I'll have to go uphill. But never mind! We'll have jolly good times—the children and I—when we get to my cabin out at the Lake."

As he walked along through the storm Uncle Toby looked on each side of the road for a sight of Skyrocket. But he did not see the dog. Nor was there any answering bark in reply to the shrill whistles uttered by Uncle Toby.

"Here, Sky! Here, Skyrocket!" the old sailor would call every now and then, but no dog appeared.

"He must have jumped out away back where I stalled the car," thought Uncle Toby. "Poor dog! He'll freeze if he has to stay out all night. And I don't know what I'll do with those children if I don't find their pet for them. Skyrocket, where are you?"

On and on went Uncle Toby, through the whirling snow. He was almost back to where the car had stopped when suddenly he heard a series of barks off to one side of the road, in a clump of trees.

"That sounds like him!" exclaimed the sailor. "Hello there, Skyrocket!" he cried.

The barking became louder. Uncle Toby floundered through the drifts, off the road and over toward the clump of evergreen trees. As he neared them a dog came dashing out, capering about in the fluffy drifts.

"Hello, Skyrocket! I've found you all right!" said Uncle Toby. "But what in the world are you doing back here? What made you jump out of the car?"

All the answer Skyrocket made was to bark. He leaped about Uncle Toby and seemed very glad to see him. But when the man started back toward the road, thinking the dog would follow, Skyrocket only barked more loudly and raced back toward the clump of trees.

"What's the matter? Is there some other dog back there you'd rather play with than come to the Curlytops?" asked the old sailor. "What's the idea?"

Skyrocket acted in such a queer way that Uncle Toby turned back to see what the matter was. And this was just what the wise dog seemed to want, for he wagged his tail joyfully and raced back ahead of Uncle Toby.

When the old sailor reached the clump of trees, under the heavy branches of which the snow was not so thick, he heard a faint mewing sound.

"Bless my heart! A kitten!" cried Uncle Toby.

And a kitten it was! A dear, cute, little kitten, half way up one of the trees, cuddled down in the thick, green branches.

"Well, no wonder you didn't want to come back and leave this poor little kitten here in the cold and storm," said kind Uncle Toby. "You're a good dog, Skyrocket!"

At this Skyrocket wagged his tail harder than ever, so it seemed a wonder that it did not fly off, and his throat must have ached with all the barking he did.

The kitten mewed and stood up when it saw Uncle Toby. It did not appear to be afraid of Skyrocket, who was capering around on the ground under the tree.

"I'll get you down and take you back with me," said the old sailor. "Come on, pussy! I don't know where I am going to get any milk to give you until we get to my place in Pocono. But I guess you'll stand it until then. I wonder how you got out here in the woods all alone?"

There was no way of finding this out, and there was no house near from which the little kitten might have wandered. Uncle Toby had an idea it might have been lost out of some car in which some children, like the Curlytops, had been riding. Then the little animal wandered into the clump of evergreens for shelter, and Skyrocket had trailed it there. The dog had probably discovered the pussy as he was racing around after he had slipped out of the car, unseen by the children or Uncle Toby.

"But you'll be all right now," said the kind old sailor. "Come to me, pussy!"

The kitten arched its back, seeming glad of a chance to stretch after being cramped on the limb. Reaching up, Uncle Toby lifted it down and put it snugly in the pocket of his big overcoat.

"Well, I wonder if you'll come back with me now?" asked Uncle Toby of Skyrocket, when the kitten had been rescued.

Skyrocket seemed very willing, for he no longer hung back, but followed with joyful barks and waggings of his tail as Uncle Toby strode through the storm with the kitten he had rescued.

It was hard work tramping back up the hill through the storm and drifts of snow with the wind blowing in his face, but the old sailor managed it, and soon the Curlytops and their friends, who had been anxiously watching through the back window, saw him looming into view.

"Here comes Uncle Toby!" cried Jan, who was the first to spy him.

"Has he got Skyrocket?" asked Ted.

"Yes, I see him!" said Tom. "He's got your dog all right."

A little later Uncle Toby was knocking the snow off his shoes on the running board of the car, and soon he was safely inside with the dog.

"Where was he?" Ted wanted to know. "What were you doing back there, Skyrocket?" he asked his pet.

"He was guarding this," said Uncle Toby, and out of his pocket came the little kitten.

"Oh! Oh!" murmured Lola. "Isn't it a darling!"

"How cute! Oh, what a dear!" exclaimed Jan.

"My kitten! Mine!" cried Trouble, always ready to claim any new pet he saw.

"Did you really find it?" asked Tom, as Jan took the kitten into her lap while she and Lola rubbed it, Trouble getting an occasional finger or two on the soft fur.

"Skyrocket found it, and I got it down out of the tree," explained the old sailor, with a laugh. "Now I guess we can move along again. I wish we had some milk foryou," he went on, looking at the little cat. "But we'll be home before dark—if we have good luck," he added, as he glanced out into the storm.

Once again the automobile started, with a new passenger on board. Skyrocket was used to cats, and after he had taken part in the rescue of the kitten he paid no more attention to it but curled up and went to sleep. As for the kitten, it did not seem to mind the dog in the least.

"I guess it isn't very hungry, Uncle Toby," said Jan in a low voice, after they had ridden several miles. "See, it's going to sleep."

And the little kitten, with eyes closed, was curled contentedly in her lap.

Uncle Toby's main thought now was to drive as fast as he could with safety, so he would get the children to his home in Pocono before the storm grew any worse and before night came.

Once in his house at Pocono they could remain until the weather cleared before going out to the cabin at Crystal Lake to spend the holidays.

They passed through a small town, and Jan suggested they might stop and get some milk for the kitten, which had awakened, and was mewing a little.

"I think we'd better not stop now," said Mr. Bardeen. "It is better for the pussy to be a little hungry for a time than for us to get stuck in the snow with night coming on. We'd all be hungry then. We'll soon be home."

They came to a railroad track, almost hidden under the snow, and Uncle Toby stopped the automobile, and, opening the door a little way, seemed to be listening.

"What's the matter?" asked Ted.

"I wanted to hear if the train was coming," was the answer. "One is due here about now, and I didn't want to cross the tracks if it was too near. But I guess it's late on account of the storm. It will be safe to cross."

He drove over the tracks and was just speeding up again when they all heard a distant whistle.

"There's the train!" exclaimed Tom.

Then came several more whistles, long toots and short toots in such a queer combination that they all knew something must be the matter.

"Maybe there's been an accident," said Ted.

"Maybe," agreed Uncle Toby. "But I think that the train is stuck in a deep cut not far from here. The cut may be filled with snow so the train can't get through. It's probably stalled there."

"Will anybody be hurt?" asked Janet.

"No, only delayed for a while. Men will come with shovels to dig out the train. We can soon see what has happened, for the auto road passes near the railroad cut."

A little later they saw that what Uncle Toby had guessed at had come to pass. The children saw a passenger train with the front part of the engine buried deep in a pile of snow that filled a cut between two rocky hills on either side of the track.

As the automobile came in sight of the train the engineer blew several more shrill whistles, waking up Skyrocket, who began to bark loudly.

CHAPTER IX

NEW PLAYMATES

"Just hear him toot!" cried Jan, putting her hands over her ears, for the automobile was now quite close to the train stuck in the big snow drift. The drift was much deeper here than at any other point along the railroad, because the narrow cut between the high rocks held the white flakes tightly packed.

"Sounds as if it was calling us," said Lola.

"I believe it is!" exclaimed Ted, as the toots of the whistle kept up. "Do you s'pose he could want us to help him, Uncle Toby?"

"How could an auto pull a stalled train out of a snowdrift?" asked Tom.

"Course we couldn't *pull* the train," admitted Ted. "But we could sort of—now— do *something*, couldn't we, Uncle Toby?" he asked.

"I believe we could, and I think that is what the engineer is trying to signal us for," was the answer. "I know this railroad cut. It is a bad place in a storm. Often trains have been stuck here for days. The engine would ram its pilot, or cowcatcher, into a drift, then snow would pile up behind the last car and the train couldn't go ahead or back up."

"Maybe that's happened now!" exclaimed Lola.

"I shouldn't be a bit surprised," said Uncle Toby.

"But what do the passengers do when the train is stuck, like this one is now?" Tom wanted to know.

"Oh, sometimes they get out and walk, as it isn't very far to the station. Or if they have something to eat, and can keep warm in the cars, they stay there until men come with shovels to dig out the train. I guess that's what this engineer wants me for—to go on to the station and have a gang of men sent to dig out his train. We'll soon find out," Uncle Toby remarked.

The automobile road ran close to the tracks and near the deep cut which was filled with snow. The storm was getting worse, but on the level there was not yet enough snow to have stopped a train. It was only in the cut that the drift was deep enough for this.

Uncle Toby stopped the automobile as near the stalled train as he could go, and waited. Soon the engineer and a man with gold braid on his cap came floundering through the deep snow at the side of the train until they were within calling distance of Uncle Toby, who opened the car door to listen.

"Could you oblige us by going to the next station and having the telegraph operator send word to headquarters that we're stalled?" asked the man with the gold braid on his cap. He was the conductor of the train.

"Yes, I'll do that for you," said Uncle Toby. "I thought you were whistling for help," he added to the engineer.

"That's what I was," came the answer. "I saw you just in time. 'Tisn't often that an auto has to come to the help of a steam engine, but it happened this time," he added, with a smile.

"Is there anything else I can do for you?" asked Uncle Toby, as he prepared to start off again. The station was a little out of his way, but he didn't mind that.

"Well, I don't know," replied the conductor slowly. "We haven't many passengers on board, and all except a little boy and girl who are on their way to Pocono will be all right. The way it is now we'll hardly get there to-night, or anyhow, not until late, and they are traveling alone. They expect to be met at Pocono by—let me see—I have his name here somewhere," and he began searching among the papers in his pocket. "The children are in my charge," he went on. "Their mother had to go to a hospital and—"

"She did?" cried Uncle Toby so suddenly that the engineer and conductor looked at him in surprise. "Is the name of the man who was to meet these children Mr. Toby Bardeen?" went on the old sailor.

"Why, yes, that's his name. I have it here on a piece of paper," said the conductor. "But how did you—"

"Are those children Harry and Mary Benton?" went on Uncle Toby.

"Those are their names, certainly," the conductor admitted. "But how in the world—"

"I'm Mr. Toby Bardeen," interrupted the old sailor. "Uncle Toby is what the Curlytops call me. I was expecting these children, but I had no idea they'd arrive so soon. It's only by chance that I'm passing this way. I didn't expect Mary and Harry for nearly a week."

"Well, the society that gave them in my charge, to see that they got safely to Pocono and to Mr. Bardeen, told me their mother had to go to the hospital sooner than she expected," reported the conductor. "I was going to telegraph you when I got to the next station to make sure you'd be on hand. They said—that is, the lady of the Fresh Air Society said she'd written you to expect the children earlier."

"Well, I didn't get the letter, because I left home to go to visit the Curlytops," said Uncle Toby. "However, it's all right now. I'll take the children right into the auto with me and soon have them home. It's lucky I met you."

"Very lucky, indeed!" agreed the conductor. "I'll go back and get the children ready for you. Poor little things, they're quite sad and forlorn. Their father was killed in the war, I understand."

"Yes," agreed Uncle Toby. "At least he's missing, and I guess he must be killed or they'd have heard something from him by this time. However, I'll take charge of the children. I used to know their mother many years ago, but I haven't seen her for some time."

"If you'll drive along the road, around the cut, to the rear of the train, the snow won't be so deep for the children," said the engineer. "I'll help you carry them out," he added to the conductor.

The rocky cut, in which the train was stuck in the snow drift, was about twice as long as the engine and cars, and in front of the cut, as well as behind it, the snow was not very deep, though it was getting deeper all the while as the white flakes came sifting down faster.

Uncle Toby started the automobile again, going to the rear of the train, as near to it as he could get. A little later the conductor and engineer came tramping through the drifts, each man carrying a child, the conductor with the girl and the engineer with the boy. The children were so wrapped up in shawls that it could scarcely be told which was the boy and which was the girl.

"There you are, my dear!" said the conductor, as he set his passenger down inside the automobile.

"And one more!" added the kind-faced but grimy engineer, putting the little boy in next to his sister.

"Is this Pocono?" the boy asked freeing himself from the shawl that wrapped him. "The lady said we weren't to get out except at Pocono."

"And we want Uncle Toby," added the girl.

"Bless your hearts, I'm Uncle Toby!" cried Mr. Bardeen. "This isn't exactly Pocono, but you'd never get there to-night if you stayed on that train. I'm going to take you off and drive you to my home in Pocono in this auto. See, here are the Curlytops and some other playmates for you," for now the two strangers could see the Curlytops and their friends, Tom and Lola.

"Curlytops!" exclaimed Harry Benton, wonderingly.

"It's on account of our hair," explained Ted, taking off his cap.

"Oh, I see!" laughed Mary. "It's lovely hair! I wish mine curled."

"I'm glad mine doesn't," her brother exclaimed. "It's too hard to comb."

"It is hard," admitted Jan, while Trouble stared open-mouthed at the new playmates.

"Is he a Curlytop, too?" asked Mary, looking at Baby William.

"He belongs to the family, but his hair doesn't curl," said Uncle Toby, with a laugh. "But now that I have you children safe in here I'd better be going," he added. "I'll tell the telegraph operator to send you help as soon as he can," he added to the engineer and the conductor, who started back to the stalled train.

"Please do," begged the conductor. "We'd like to get dug out of here before night."

"Isn't it lovely in here, Harry?" asked Mary Benton, looking around inside the comfortable automobile.

"I should say so!" he exclaimed. "I never was in a car like this before."

The two children were poor—one need but look at their clothes to see this. But they were clean and neat.

"And, oh, look! A dog!" cried Harry.

"That's Skyrocket! He likes you," said Ted, for the dog, after sniffing at the two new playmates, wagged his tail in friendly fashion.

"I like him!" said Harry.

"And, oh, look at the kitten!" cried Mary, reaching her hand down to pat the little bunch of fur that was purring on the seat between Lola and Jan.

"Uncle Toby just found it in the woods," Jan explained.

"What's its name?" asked Mary.

"We haven't named it yet," Ted answered. "Skyrocket saw it up a tree and barked."

"I think Fluff would be a nice name for the pussy," said Mary. "He's such a fluffy ball of fur."

"Oh, that would be a lovely name!" cried Lola. "Why don't you call it that?"

"I guess we will. You may name the kitten Fluff, Mary, and it'll be part your cat."

"Oh, how nice!" murmured the poor little girl. "I never had even part of a cat before."

"Uncle Toby has a cat and his name is Snuff!" said Trouble. "An' he's got a monkey and a parrot!"

Mary and Harry looked as though they did not know whether or not to believe this. Seeing the doubt on their faces Ted exclaimed:

"That's right! Uncle Toby has a lot of pets out at his place, and we're going to take them to Crystal Lake with us, aren't we, Uncle Toby?"

"Oh, I guess if we take your dog that will be enough," chuckled the old sailor. "The others will be better off in Pocono. But you'll have a chance to see them," he added to the new children, noticing how disappointed they looked. Then Harry and Mary smiled.

"Well, I must be getting on if I'm going to send help to the people on the stalled train," remarked Uncle Toby, as he turned the automobile around. "And then we'll go on to Pocono. Aunt Sallie will be getting anxious about us."

"Is Aunt Sallie a monkey or a parrot?" Harry asked.

"Neither one!" answered Uncle Toby, with a laugh, in which the Curlytops joined. "She's my housekeeper; and she'll go with us to Crystal Lake for the holidays."

"What will you do with your pets?" asked Ted.

"I'll get some one to look after them. I haven't as many as when you Curlytops played circus with them. But there's enough. Too many, so Aunt Sallie thinks."

It was not a very long ride to the station from where word could be sent that help was needed by the stalled train. The agent promised to telegraph for snow shovelers at once.

Uncle Toby was about to drive on again when Janet stopped him by saying:

"Maybe the station agent could give us a little milk for the pussy."

"Maybe he could," agreed the old sailor. "I'll ask him."

As it happened, the agent kept a cat in the station on account of the mice, and that day he had brought a little milk for his pet—more milk than Choo-Choo, as he called his cat, wanted.

"I'll give you some for your pussy," said the agent, after he had telegraphed for the snow shovelers.

I wish you could have seen Fluff lap up the milk, which was warmed for him and put in a saucer on the floor of the automobile. He was hungry—was the little stray kitten that had come down out of the evergreen tree—and his little sides seemed to swell out like balloons as he lapped up every drop of milk.

"I hope your cat Choo-Choo won't get hungry," said Jan, as the last of the milk disappeared.

"I can get him some more," said the agent. "Anyhow, he isn't as hungry as your pussy was."

"Good-bye!" called Uncle Toby, as he started off once more. "I hope the stalled passengers will soon be shoveled out."

"I guess they will be," the agent said.

It was almost dark when the big automobile reached the village of Pocono where Uncle Toby lived.

"Now we'll soon be snug and warm," he told the children. "I have more of a load than when I started, but I'm glad I found you two," he said to Mary and Harry. "You're going to have a good time with my Curlytops."

Harry and Mary, who had never had much of a good time in all their lives, were beginning to be happy. They had been very small when their father went off to war— they hardly remembered him, in fact. Mr. Benton need not have gone, had he wished to stay at home, for he could have been excused, or have done some other war work than fighting. But he was a brave man and wanted to do his best for his country. So he had gone to France. After awhile he was missing, and though his wife was helped by her friends and by the government, still she had hard work to get along and there was not much money with which to give Mary and Harry good times. But happier days were ahead of them.

"There's Uncle Toby's house!" cried Ted, as the automobile turned into the driveway.

"Oh, but something has happened!" exclaimed Jan. "Look! There's a crowd out in front!"

And surely enough, a throng of people could be seen standing in the dusk and storm in front of Uncle Toby's home.

CHAPTER X

AMONG THE PETS

As the automobile driven by Uncle Toby and containing the Curlytops and their playmates came to a stop near the side entrance to Mr. Bardeen's house, the door opened, letting out a stream of light on the white snow.

"Is that the police?" asked a voice which Ted remembered as that of Mrs. Watson, or "Aunt Sallie," as Uncle Toby called her.

"No, this isn't the police," Uncle Toby answered, through the half-opened door of the car that Ted had unlatched, ready to leap out.

Aunt Sallie did not seem to know Uncle Toby's voice, for she asked another question.

"Is it the firemen then?"

"Good gracious!" cried Uncle Toby, opening the automobile door wider, so that a swirl of snow drifted in. "What in the world is the matter? Why do you want the firemen and policemen, Aunt Sallie?"

"Oh, thank goodness! It's you, is it, Uncle Toby?"

"Yes! Yes!" was the quick answer. "You stay in the car a moment, children," said Mr. Bardeen, as he got out on the side of the steering wheel. "Something must have happened. I'll see what it is."

Just then the crowd, which stood partly in the street and partly in the yard of Uncle Toby's house, but up at the farther end, away from the driveway, gave a shout.

"There he goes!" cried several voices.

"What can have happened?" exclaimed Janet, greatly excited.

"It's a fire, I guess," said Ted. "Aunt Sallie was asking for the firemen."

"And she asked for the policemen, too," said Tom. "Maybe it's a burglar up on the roof."

"That's right!" chimed in Harry, the new boy. "And maybe he's trying to go down the chimney."

"Like Santa Claus," added his sister Mary, whom Jan and Lola had begun to like very much.

"I want to see Santa C'aus!" cried Trouble, and he made a wiggle to get out of the open door by which Uncle Toby had left.

"No! No!" cried Ted, catching hold of his little brother.

"Something has happened, anyhow," decided Tom. "This crowd wouldn't be here for nothing. But I don't believe it's a fire, for there isn't any smoke. I guess the reason Aunt Sallie wanted the firemen was because they have ladders to get somebody down off the roof."

"Who could be up on the roof?" Jan wanted to know.

No one answered, but as both front doors of the closed automobile were now open the children could hear what Uncle Toby and Aunt Sallie were saying.

"What in the world has happened?" asked Uncle Toby.

"It's Jack, your monkey," was the answer. "He got loose a little while ago and scrambled up on the roof. He's perched there now, near the chimney. First I knew of it was when I saw a lot of boys in front of the house, looking up. I thought the chimney was on fire."

"Was that why you wanted the firemen?" asked Uncle Toby.

"Partly," answered Aunt Sallie. "I telephoned for the fire department, and when I heard your automobile in the side yard I thought it was the firemen."

"But why did you send for the firemen when you found out the chimney wasn't burning?" Uncle Toby asked.

"I thought they could get the monkey down with ladders," was the housekeeper's reply.

"Then why did you send for the police?" went on Uncle Toby.

"To keep the crowd in order," sighed Aunt Sallie. "Oh, I've had such a time! Some of the boys cut up so, and threw snowballs at Jack."

"My goodness! That's so, it is snowing!" cried Uncle Toby, as if, for the time, he had forgotten all about it. "Poor Jack will catch his death of cold up there on the roof in the storm. How did he get out? Never mind; don't tell me now! I must get him down before he gets pneumonia. Monkeys are very likely to get that if they get a chill."

"I don't believe he'll get cold," said Aunt Sallie. "He has a coat on."

"A coat on? Whose coat?"

"One of your old ones," answered Aunt Sallie. "He grabbed it up off the rack as he scrambled out of the window and climbed the rain-water pipe to the roof. If any one can get him down, you can, Uncle Toby."

"Yes, I guess I can. Jack always minds me. But it's hard to see him in the dark."

"Oh, the electric light in front shines right on the roof," replied Aunt Sallie. "And as the roof is white with snow, Jack shows quite plain. Do get him down so the crowd will go away."

"Are the rest of the pets all right?" asked Mr. Bardeen.

"Yes," said Aunt Sallie, and the listening children were glad to hear this.

"Come on in, Curlytops!" called Uncle Toby from the side porch. "There isn't anything serious the matter. Jack has just gotten up on the roof, that's all. It isn't the first time, for he often does it in summer, but I never knew him to go out in the cold before. I guess he wants to show that he'd be all right for taking out to CrystalLake, but I'm not going to humor him. Come on in Curlytops and the rest of you children!"

Out of the car scrambled the children, eager to see and hear all that was going on. They had hardly more than reached the porch than out in front of Uncle Toby's house sounded a rapidly clanging bell.

"Oh, here comes firemans! Here comes firemans!" shouted Trouble, jumping up and down in delight.

And, surely enough, in the electrically lighted street could be seen the glittering fire engine and the hook and ladder truck, with prancing horses which seemed to delight being out in the storm.

There was a roaring murmur from the crowd, and Uncle Toby looked at Aunt Sallie and shook his head.

"You surely have caused some excitement around here," he said, but he could not help laughing.

"I go see fire engines!" cried Trouble. "I go!"

"You'll stay right here with me!" declared Jan, taking a firm hold of her little brother's arm.

"No! Don't want to!" shouted Trouble. "Wants go see fire engines! I 'ikes fire engines!"

He squirmed and struggled so that it seemed as if he would break away from Janet. Uncle Toby and Aunt Sallie had gone around to the front of the house to meet some of the firemen who were asking where the blaze was as they did not see any smoke.

"Be good, Trouble!" begged Lola, trying to help Janet manage the little fellow, who was tired and cross from the long day's ride.

"Want to see fire engines!" he insisted, for the engine and truck were now out of view from the side porch, having drawn up farther along the street.

"Oh, maybe the police wagon will come and you can see it from here," added Mary, trying to do her best to aid in soothing William.

This seemed to quiet him at once. He was just a little afraid of a policeman.

And, surely enough, just then the police patrol wagon, with its clanging bell, not quite as loud as the fire engine, though, came up and a number of officers jumped out. There was another roar from the crowd as this added excitement was provided. Never had there been such an evening in Pocono, with the big storm getting worse all the while.

But Uncle Toby took charge of matters. He explained to the police and the firemen what had happened—that Aunt Sallie had become so excited she had summoned more help than she had really needed.

"But is there really a monkey up on the roof?" asked a policeman.

"Yes, my monkey Jack is up there near the chimney," said Mr. Bardeen. "You can see him. He's got on one of my coats."

Without a doubt there was Jack, sitting on the ridge of the roof, one hairy paw thrust through an arm of the coat, clinging to the bricks of the chimney.

"I'd like to get him down," said Uncle Toby, "for he is a valuable animal, and he may take cold and get pneumonia even if he has on a coat."

"Well, we're the boys to get him down," laughed one of the firemen. "But will he bite?" he asked anxiously. "I don't know much about monkeys, but I guess they can bite."

"Jack won't; that is, not after I speak to him," said Uncle Toby. "I'll call him to come down, and you can go up on a ladder and get him if you will."

"Oh, we'll do it all right," said the fireman. He and the police officers knew and liked Uncle Toby.

Shortly afterward a ladder was raised to the roof, and a fireman went up. He had to be careful on the sloping roof, on account of the slippery snow that covered it. But another ladder, laid on the shingles, gave him a firm footing.

Nearer and nearer he crawled to the crouching monkey. The crowd, which had been laughing and joking, kept quiet now so Uncle Toby could talk to Jack.

"Come on down, old fellow! Let the fireman bring you down. And don't bite him!" called Uncle Toby to his pet.

Jack seemed to understand. He chattered a little, and then, when the fireman was near enough, the monkey put his arms around the man's neck and clung tightly.

"Now you're all right, old chap!" said the fireman, who was fond of animals. "I've got you!"

A little later man and monkey were safe on the ground, while the crowd cheered. Uncle Toby took Jack from the fireman, and the monkey nestled in his master's arms, seemingly very glad to be down off the roof and out of the storm.

"I must get him some hot milk to drink," said Uncle Toby, as the firemen and police started back to their quarters. The crowd, seeing that there was to be no more excitement, melted away out of the storm.

"Come, Curlytops, get in the house! All of you get in the house out of the storm!" cried Uncle Toby, for the children had gone around to the front to watch the rescue of Jack.

"Yes, yes! Come in!" cried Aunt Sallie. "You'll all get your deaths of sneezes! Talk about hot milk for a monkey! I guess these children need it more than Jack does!"

"We'll all have some hot milk!" declared Uncle Toby. "Here, Aunt Sallie, you look after the Curlytops and their friends while I put the car away, and then I'll come back and we'll have a cozy supper," went on Mr. Bardeen. "I'll put Jack by the fire to thaw him out."

"I'm hungry!" announced Trouble.

"Bless your heart! you shall have something to eat as soon as I can get it on the table," said Aunt Sallie. "That bad old Jack made a lot of work!"

She shook a finger at the monkey, who whimpered a little.

"Oh, don't scold him!" begged Lola.

"Will he do tricks?" asked Tom.

"He's done enough tricks for one night," replied Aunt Sallie, as she bustled about to get supper, while Uncle Toby put the car out of the storm.

"Take off your hat, Mary," suggested Jan to the new girl, who stood about a bit shyly.

Before the little girl could do this her hat was suddenly snatched from her head, and a harsh voice cried:

"Eat 'em up! Eat 'em up! Eat 'em all up!"

"Oh! Oh!" screamed Mary. "What is it?"

"Don't be afraid!" laughed Ted. "You're just among Uncle Toby's pets!"

CHAPTER XI

WHERE DID TROUBLE GO?

Mary Benton, the little girl whose father had gone to the Big War and had never been heard of since, was really frightened by the screeching voice and by feeling her hat snatched off in that strange way. Even what Ted said about being among Uncle Toby's pets did not seem to make her feel any better.

She turned quickly around, and saw her hat that had been snatched off in the black beak of a big red and green bird which was perched on the back of a chair.

"Dat's Mr. Nip!" announced Trouble. He knew the parrot from the previous summer.

"Eat 'em up! Eat 'em up! Eat 'em all up!" croaked Mr. Nip in his harsh voice.

"Well, please don't eat Mary's hat up!" laughed Jan. "She'll want it to wear when we go to Crystal Lake."

"Is that parrot going to the Lake with us?" asked Lola.

"If he does I'll have to be careful of my hat," added Mary, who was getting over her fright. "It's a new one," she went on, and the other girls rightly guessed that, being very poor, Mary did not have many hats. Then and there Lola and Jan made up their minds to be kind to Mary, whose mother was in the hospital and whose father—well, no one knew what had happened to him.

"Here are some more pets!" cried jolly Uncle Toby, as he came in out of the storm, having put the car in his barn. He was followed by Skyrocket, who barked and leaped about, shaking snow-flakes all about. In his arms Uncle Toby carried Fluff, the little kitten that had been rescued from a "Ch'is'mus tree," as Trouble called the evergreen.

"Oh, we forgot all about him!" exclaimed Jan, as she took the little stranger from Uncle Toby.

"It wouldn't be wonderful if you forgot even your names," laughed Uncle Toby, "considering all the excitement that was going on when we got here. But we're all right now, I guess."

SHE TURNED AND SAW HER HAT IN THE BEAK OF A BIG RED AND GREEN BIRD.

Skyrocket went over to sniff around Jack, the monkey, with which pet the Curlytops' dog was well acquainted, so the two soon became friendly.

"I guess he misses Tip and Top," observed Ted, speaking of the two valuable trick poodles, which had been sold since the children found them in the show, after they had been stolen.

"Well, there are plenty of other animals," said Aunt Sallie, as she finished setting the table and called to the children to take their places.

Such a jolly time as followed! The Curlytops and their playmates, the new as well as the old ones, were all hungry from their ride through the cold. Even Trouble forgot about being sleepy while he ate, and if Mary and Harry remembered about their mother in the hospital that thought did not chase away the smiles from their faces.

At times, on the trip, Ted and Jan had given some thought to matters at home, and had wondered if Daddy Martin would lose so much money as to make the family poor. But now Ted and his sister were having a good time with the others.

Jack, the monkey, seemed to have gotten over the slight shivering caused by foolishly going up on the roof in the storm, and he and Skyrocket ate their meal behind the warm stove on one side, while Snuff, Uncle Toby's big cat, and Fluff, the new kitten, lapped warm milk from the same saucer on the other side of the stove.

As for Mr. Nip, the parrot, he seemed satisfied after he had pulled off Mary's hat, and he was now asleep with his head under his wing, perched on his stand in one corner.

"How did Jack get out, Aunt Sallie?" asked Uncle Toby, as knives and forks began to slow up a little in the supper race, the children becoming less hungry the more they ate.

"I had left a window open, and he seemed to know it," was the answer. "I never knew it to fail that if I left a window open so much as a crack but what he'd find it. He's the smartest monkey I ever saw! But he's a rascal just the same!"

"Well, you'll have a little rest from all the pets, except maybe Skyrocket," said Uncle Toby. "We'll take him with us out to Crystal Lake, but the other pets we'll leave here."

Uncle Toby's house was a large one and had plenty of beds in it for the children. It was warm and cozy, and Aunt Sallie had seen to it that everything should be comfortable for the Curlytops and their playmates.

"I thought you two were coming by train," she said to Mary and Harry, when supper was over and the plans for the night began to be talked about.

"They were on the train. But I took them off when it became stuck in the snow," explained Uncle Toby. "I hope they have dug the engine out by this time. If they haven't it may have to stay there a long time, for this storm is getting worse."

The children thought so too, as they listened to the wind howling around the corners of the house and down the chimney, while the hard flakes of snow beat against the windows.

But they were snug and warm in Uncle Toby's house, and Jan and her brother, with Lola and Tom, were so jolly, suggesting so many games to play and talking about the good times to come at Crystal Lake, that though Mary and Harry had begun to feel homesick this soon wore off, and the strange playmates laughed with their new friends.

Trouble was to sleep in a big bed with Jan in a room next to Aunt Sallie. And in the same room with Jan and her little brother, Mary and Lola would sleep, but in separate beds.

The three older boys had a room to themselves, each with a single bed, so they would not disturb one another.

"And mind!" cried Uncle Toby, when the time came to "turn in," as a soldier or a sailor might say. "Mind! No pillow fights!"

"Oh, no!" cried Tom and Ted, winking at each other.

And I think Uncle Toby must have known that they would have a little fun in this way. For he did not come up to stop them when they began tossing about at each other the soft, fluffy pillows. At this game there was a jolly good time for half an hour.

But even boys can get tired sometimes, and these boys had had a long automobile ride that day. So they finally gave up tossing the pillows about and settled down snugly in their beds. The girls and Trouble had gone to sleep long before this.

"Well, you certainly have quite a houseful, Uncle Toby," said Aunt Sallie that night, when locking-up time came, "with seven children, to say nothing of the animals."

"Oh, I like 'em all!" exclaimed the old sailor, with a laugh. "And I just had to take the Curlytops. There was no place for them to go when their father and mother had to start off on that trip. As for Tom and Lola, I wanted the Curlytops to have some playmates over the holidays. And about Mary and Harry—well, I couldn't leave them in the big city all alone, with their mother in the hospital."

"No, I suppose not. Poor children! Poor Mother! I hope she gets better!"

"I hope so, too," said Uncle Toby. "And I hope the Curlytops' father doesn't lose his money."

Janet was awakened early the next morning by feeling something cold on her face. She was dreaming that Jack, the monkey, was still up on the roof, but that he had a long tail which reached all the way to the ground. And she dreamed that Jack was dipping his tail in ice water and tickling her on the cheek.

Something almost like this was happening as Janet opened her eyes, for she saw Trouble bending over her with a lump of snow in his fist, rubbing the cold stuff on her nose.

"Oh, Trouble! Stop it!" cried Janet, rolling over in bed and giving her brother a little push. He dropped some of the cold snow down her neck. "Oh!" screamed Jan. "You're freezing me!"

"You shouldn't have jiggled me!" complained Trouble, whose grasp on the snowball had been loosened as his sister moved. "I wanted you open your eyes," he added.

"I guess you made her open them all right," laughed Lola from her bed, next to Janet's.

The talking aroused Mary, who sat up, rubbing her eyes.

"Oh, where am I?" she exclaimed. "I—Oh, I remember!" she said. "I was dreaming I was back home!"

"And I was dreaming Jack was slapping me with his tail wet in ice water," laughed Janet. "Then I wake up and find Trouble with a snowball. Where did you get it?" she asked, tossing the half-melted lump into the water basin near by.

"It blowed in the window," Trouble explained, pointing to more of the white flakes on the sill. They had drifted in around a crack.

"You mustn't get out of bed and run around in your bare feet," said Janet. "I wonder what sort of a day it is?" She slipped on her little robe and slippers and went to the window, meanwhile covering Trouble warmly in bed. "It's stopped snowing," she said, "and the sun is out. We can make snowmen, big snowballs, and everything."

"Oh, what fun it will be!" cried Lola.

"Snow in the country is much nicer than in the city where I live," said Mary. "It seems to stay clean longer out here."

Meanwhile Ted, Tom, and Harry had also discovered that there was a chance for plenty of fun out of doors. They were soon up and getting dressed, and when Aunt Sallie had seen that Trouble was washed and dressed all the children went down to breakfast.

"Where are all the pets?" asked Mary, seeing only Mr. Nip perched on his stand, cracking seeds in his strong beak.

"They're having their breakfasts out in their room," said Aunt Sallie, for a special room had been provided for the animals.

A little later the Curlytops and their playmates were having fun in the snow outside, Skyrocket romping around with them. There were sleds at Uncle Toby's house, and not far from it a little hill, and on this the children were soon coasting.

"It's more fun than our toboggan," cried Ted.

"Yes, it is. But the snow isn't going to last long," observed Tom. "It's too warm."

"It's melting now," added Harry.

Indeed the warm sun would soon make short work of this first snow, which had come much earlier than usual. The children made up their minds to have as much fun as they could while it lasted.

So they coasted, they made snowmen, rolled big snowballs and the boys even started to build a snow fort, for the white flakes were wet enough to pack well and stay in place once they were piled up.

Trouble played with the others, sometimes getting in the way and toppling down, to pick himself up again and fall down once more.

"I havin' 'ots of fun!" he laughed.

In fact all the children were—so much so that they hardly wanted to come in to lunch. But playing out in the air made them hungry, and soon they were eagerly eating.

"How soon are we going to Crystal Lake?" asked Ted of Uncle Toby, as the Curlytops and the others prepared to rush out in the snow once more.

"Oh, we'll go in a few days," was the answer. "Might as well wait for this snow to melt, as it's bound to if this weather keeps up. It will be easier going for the auto then, as the roads to the Lake are rather rough."

"Well, we're having fun here," chuckled Ted, as he ran out to join his playmates.

"Let's make a big fort!" proposed Tom, for they had made a little one, and trampled it down in having a "battle."

"All right," agreed the other boys.

"I he'p!" offered Trouble.

"No you'll only be in the way," Ted replied. "You go over and help sister make a snowman," he added, for this is what Jan and the other two girls were trying to do.

This was a bit selfish on Ted's part, for he must have known that Trouble would annoy his sister as much as the little fellow would be in the way of himself and his chums. But brothers are this way sometimes, I suppose.

Anyhow, Trouble toddled off to see if he could not play with Jan, Lola, and Mary. He saw them shaping the snowman.

"I he'p!" he offered, trying to put a little ball on the snowman's coat to serve as a "button."

"Oh, Trouble! Don't!" begged Jan. "Go over and play with the boys! You'll spoil our snowman!"

"Ted told me come here!" announced William.

Poor Trouble! No one seemed to want him!

"Oh, let him stay," begged Mary, "I'll watch him."

"All right," sighed Jan. She was trying to make the snowman's face, and it was not easy work.

Just how it happened no one seemed to know but the boys forgot all about Trouble in the excitement of making their fort. And though Mary had promised to keep watch over the little fellow she forgot when she went to the shed to get two pieces of coal to make eyes for the snowman.

It was not until after the snowman was finished and Ted had shouted what fun it would be if they could put him in the fort that Trouble was missed.

"Where is he?" asked Janet, looking around the yard.

"He was here a little while ago," said Lola.

"I saw him too," added Tom.

But now Trouble was not in sight.

"Maybe he went into the house to get something to eat," suggested Mary.

Jan ran to the door and asked Aunt Sallie.

"Why, no," she answered. "Trouble didn't come in here!"

"Oh, where can Trouble be?" half sobbed Janet.

CHAPTER XII

OFF TO CRYSTAL LAKE

This was not the first time Trouble Martin had been lost or missing. It happened more or less often at home in Cresco, and once when the Curlytops had come to Uncle Toby's. But he had never before been lost after a big snow storm—that is, as far as Janet or Teddy could remember. What Janet was afraid of was that her little brother might wander off and fall into some drift. For the snow was deep in places not very far from Uncle Toby's house.

"Oh, we'll find him!" declared Ted. "He can't be far off. We didn't want him playing around our fort for fear he'd spoil it."

"And I sent him away from our snowman on the same account," sighed Janet. "I wish I had kept him by me."

Aunt Sallie came out of the house, her apron thrown over her head.

"Did you find Trouble?" she asked.

"No'm," chorused the children.

"Dear me!" exclaimed the old lady. "You must call Uncle Toby and tell him. He's out in the barn working over the auto, getting ready for the trip to Crystal Lake. Go tell him Trouble is missing."

Janet and the others thought this would be the best thing to do, and Uncle Toby soon heard the latest happening regarding the Curlytops.

"If Trouble isn't in the house nor around where you are playing, he must have wandered off down the street," said Uncle Toby. "The walks have been pretty well cleaned off by this time. The snowplow has been along." For in Pocono the street cleaning department sent out a big snowplow, drawn by horses, after every big storm, and thus the sidewalks were made easy to walk on without waiting for each householder to clean his own space.

"But where would he go?" asked Janet, hardly able to keep back her tears.

"That's what we must find out," said Uncle Toby. "Don't worry. We'll find him. I'll ask the police if they've seen him. A little chap like Trouble would be sure to be noticed."

"Unless maybe he fell in a snowdrift," suggested Janet.

"If he fell in he'd shout and cry until some of us came to help him out," said Uncle Toby. "Now we'll start a searching party. I'll go with you girls up the street, and the three boys can go down the street. Ask every one you meet if they have seen Trouble."

"Only," suggested Jan, "we'd better give him his right name of William."

"That's so!" laughed Uncle Toby. "If we go along asking every one we meet if they have seen Trouble, they'll think we are trying to make fun of them. Yes, we must ask for news of a little boy named William."

So they started out, Ted, Tom and Harry going one way, and Uncle Toby and the three girls the other way. Aunt Sallie remained behind in the house, but she was very anxious, and she said she would call up police headquarters, asking that each officer be told to be on the lookout.

At first the question asked by the searchers had no effect. No one seemed to have noticed Trouble toddling along the streets, which, as Uncle Toby had said, were now quite free from snow, which was piled high on either side.

"Maybe he wandered off toward the woods," suggested Lola, for there was a clump of trees, called "woods" not far from Uncle Toby's house.

"I don't believe so," was Mr. Bardeen's answer. "I think he wouldn't go there alone. But here comes Policeman McCarthy. I'll ask him."

And, to the delight of the girls, Policeman McCarthy said he had seen a little boy going along the street a few minutes before.

"I don't know what his name was," the officer said. "But he was dressed just as you say. He seemed to know where he was going, so I didn't stop him, though he was pretty little to be out alone."

"Where did he go?" asked Uncle Toby.

"Right down that way," answered the policeman, pointing. "He was standing in front of that barber shop the last I saw him."

"Oh, now I know where he's gone!" suddenly cried Janet.

"Where?" asked Uncle Toby.

"In the barber shop," answered the little girl. "Trouble was in the bathroom this morning, Uncle Toby, getting washed," Janet explained. "He found some of your shaving soap, and he liked the smell of it. He was rubbing it on his face when I stopped him. He asked me where you got your soap and I told him in a barber shop, I thought. Then he wanted to know what a barber shop was like, and I told him it was a place that had a red, white, and blue pole in front of it. So that's where he's gone—to the barber shop to get some of that nice smelling soap."

"I shouldn't wonder," agreed Uncle Toby. "I hope the barber kept him there, if he went in."

They hurried to the shop in front of which was a gay red, white, and blue pole, and there they found Trouble. But they found him more than just inquiring for scented soap, for he was up in the chair, kept specially for children.

In front of Trouble, draped around his neck, was a white apron, and the barber, with comb and scissors, was just about to cut the little fellow's long hair.

"Trouble! What are you doing?" cried Uncle Toby, his voice causing the barber to turn around in surprise.

"I goin' get hair cut!" announced the little fellow.

"Oh, no! You mustn't!" exclaimed Jan.

"I wants hair cut an' nice smelly stuff on my face," announced the little fellow, holding tightly to the arms of the barber's chair, lest he be made to come out.

"No, no!" said Janet. "Not now, Trouble!"

"Didn't some of you send him to have his hair trimmed?" asked the barber, in some surprise.

"No, indeed!" laughed Uncle Toby, who knew the barber quite well. "He ran off by himself. I'm glad we reached here in time to stop you. He's a little tyke; that's what he is!"

"Well, he came in here as bold as you please," said Mr. Miller, the barber. "He climbed up in the chair himself, and though he didn't tell me so exactly, I thought he wanted a hair cut, as it's pretty long. He did say he wanted some nice perfume on him, but all the children say that when they come in here. And I've often had them as young as he is come in here alone. But of course their fathers or mothers sent 'em. And you didn't send this little chap?" he asked, as he helped Trouble down out of the chair, much to William's disgust.

"No, we didn't send him," chuckled Uncle Toby. "He just took the notion himself. Tried some of my shaving soap this morning, so his sister says. Well, I am glad he's found. We'd better take him back so the boys will know we've come to the end of the search. You mustn't do anything like this again, Trouble," said Uncle Toby, a bit sternly, shaking his finger at William.

"Nope!" he readily promised. "Maybe I have some nice smelly stuff take home?" he added hopefully.

"Here you are!" laughed the barber, and he gave Trouble a little cake of scented soap.

"You gave us a big scare," said Janet, when they were on their way back to Uncle Toby's house.

"You make big snowman?" asked Trouble, and that's about all he seemed to care. Janet wanted to laugh, but she did not think it wise.

They met the boys coming back, Ted and the other two being anxious, as of course they had heard no word about the missing wanderer. But they saw William in Uncle Toby's arms, and knew everything was now all right.

"I'll keep my eye on you after this," said Janet when the children were once more playing in the snow around Uncle Toby's house.

But it was one thing to say she would keep watch over a little chap like Trouble, and another thing actually to do it. And William made more trouble before the day was over.

Evening came, when it was time to stop playing out of doors and come into the house. And it was after supper when the children were sitting in the living room, listening to Uncle Toby tell a story, that Aunt Sallie came running in from the kitchen.

"Oh, Uncle Toby!" she cried. "There's a leak in one of the pipes. There's a big puddle of water in the middle of the kitchen floor. It was dry when I went up to see if the beds were ready, and when I came down, just now, I found a lot of water there."

"A broken pipe? That's too bad!" exclaimed Uncle Toby. "I may be able to fix it myself; but if I can't, we'll have hard work getting a plumber this time of night. I can shut off the water in the cellar, though, I suppose. However, I'll take a look."

The children followed Uncle Toby and Aunt Sallie out to the kitchen. Surely enough there was a large puddle of water in the middle of the oilcloth. Uncle Toby looked up and around, and said:

"I can't see what pipe has burst. If it was one in the kitchen the water would be spurting out now. It seems to come from under the sink."

By this time Trouble was toddling across the room toward the sink, under which was a sort of cupboard with two swinging doors. The little fellow was trying to open one of these doors.

"Here, Trouble! Let Uncle Toby look!" said Ted.

"I wants get my snowball," announced William.

"Your snowball!" cried Jan.

"Yep! I put big snowball there when I comed in. Wants to get it now," and William tugged at the sink door.

"Ha! Maybe that's where the water came from!" cried Uncle Toby.

And it was. As the sink cupboard was opened more water was seen, and in the midst of the puddle there floated what was left of a large ball of snow. Trouble had brought it in, put it under the sink when no one was looking, and there the warmth of the kitchen stove had slowly melted it, causing the water to run out under the doors.

"What in the world made you put a snowball in there, Trouble?" asked Ted, as Aunt Sallie mopped up the water.

"Maybe I wants make snowman in night," was Trouble's answer.

That may have been his reason—no one could tell. At any rate, no great harm was done, as the snow water was clean and the oilcloth was soon wiped dry.

"I guess you'd better go to bed before you get into any more mischief," said Janet.

And soon the Curlytops and their playmates were all sound asleep.

The next day it rained, and as the weather turned warm the snow was soon nearly all melted or washed away.

"So much the better for making the trip to Crystal Lake," said Uncle Toby. "I don't care what it does after we get there, but I like good going though the woods."

"Oh, what fun we'll have at Crystal Lake!" cried the Curlytops and their playmates.

They started three days later, in the big automobile. Uncle Toby, Aunt Sallie, the children, and Skyrocket. Uncle Toby hired a colored man and his wife to come and live in his house and look after the pets, including the new kitten, Fluff, while he was at camp for the holidays.

"Hurray! Here we go!" cried Ted and the others, as Uncle Toby started the automobile.

As they were turning out of the drive a boy came riding up the street on a bicycle, waving a yellow envelope in his hand.

"Wait a minute! Wait a minute!" he shouted. "Here's a telegram!"

CHAPTER XIII

THE LONELY CABIN

Uncle Toby brought the automobile to a stop and looked at the boy.

"A telegram?" repeated Uncle Toby. "For whom is it?"

"You," answered the boy, and Ted and Jan wondered if it could be about their father and mother. Suppose one of them were ill, or suppose Daddy Martin had lost all his money, and Ted and Jan had to go back home? It doesn't take much to worry children, just as it doesn't take much to make them happy.

Tom and Lola, too, knew that telegrams often bring bad news, and as Uncle Toby was opening the yellow envelope which the boy handed him, these two playmates of the Curlytops thought perhaps something had happened at their home.

And, in turn, Harry and Mary began to fear that the message might be bad news about their mother in the hospital. A few tears began to form in Mary's eyes, but they soon dried away when Uncle Toby, after reading the message, gave a hearty laugh.

"Ha! Ha! Ha!" chuckled Uncle Toby. "This is funny! The idea of sending me a message like this!"

"What is it?" asked Ted, while the messenger boy waited to see if Uncle Toby wanted to send an answer to the telegram.

"Oh, it's from an old friend of mine, Hezekiah Armstrong. He says he has a chance to buy an elephant cheap, and he telegraphs to ask me if I don't want it."

"Want an elephant!" repeated Jan.

"Yes, for a pet, I suppose. It may be one of his jokes, or he may mean it, but I certainly don't want an elephant, in winter time especially."

"Would you want one in summer?" asked Tom, with a laugh.

"Well, an elephant is easier to take care of in summer than in winter," answered Mr. Bardeen. "In warm weather I could turn the elephant out in the meadow and let him eat grass. But in winter I'd have to keep him in a barn and let him eat hay, and they eat a big lot of hay—enough to keep me poor, I guess. So I'll just telegraph back to Hezekiah that I don't want an elephant. We couldn't take it to Crystal Lake, anyhow. Here you are, son!" he called pleasantly to the boy. "You take back this message for me."

Uncle Toby wrote it on a blank of which the boy had a number in his pocket. As Mr. Bardeen paid the lad and was about to start the automobile again, the boy asked:

"Where you going?" He was acquainted with Mr. Bardeen.

"Out to Crystal Lake," answered Uncle Toby, and the children in the automobile wondered if the messenger lad did not wish he were going.

"Crystal Lake!" exclaimed the boy. "Are you going out there to catch the burglar?"

"Catch the burglar? What burglar?" asked Uncle Toby. "This is the first I've heard a burglar was out there. What do you mean?"

"It was in the paper this morning," the boy went on. "It said some of the cabins and camps out at the Lake had been broken into and robbed. They haven't any police out there, so it said the police from Pocono had been asked to see if they could catch the burglar. I thought maybe that's why you were going out."

"Oh, no!" replied Uncle Toby. "I'm not a policeman. And though I wouldn't want a burglar to get into my cabin, he wouldn't find very much to take if he did get in. I guess, most likely, it's some tramp that has broken into some of the cabins. We'll not worry about that, shall we, Curlytops?" chuckled Uncle Toby. "If we find any burglars out there we'll make Skyrocket bite 'em—sha'n't we, Trouble?" and he playfully pinched William's cheek.

"We make elephant run after 'em!" laughed Trouble.

"That's right!" said Uncle Toby.

Once more they started off in the big comfortable car that so well kept out the cold. Most of the snow from the recent storm was gone, though Uncle Toby said there would probably be some left in the woods around Crystal Lake, where it did not melt as fast as in Pocono.

"I'm glad that telegram wasn't bad news from home," said Ted. "It isn't any good to get bad news just when you start to have fun."

"That's right," agreed Tom. "My father wasn't feeling very well when we started, and I thought maybe the message was to say he was worse."

"Mary and I haven't any father to get messages from," said Harry, rather sadly. "We hardly remember him, for we were little when he went away to the war."

"And he never came back?" asked Jan softly.

"No, he never came back," repeated Mary, trying to keep the tears from her eyes.

Uncle Toby saw that the children might be made sad by this sort of talk, so, as they were passing a meat market on the edge of town, he stopped the car and began to get out.

"What are you going to do?" asked Aunt Sallie. "I have everything we need for getting supper out at the Lake, and we have our lunch with us."

"It isn't for us," said Uncle Toby. "It's for Skyrocket. I want to get him a nice bone to gnaw. It will keep him quiet on the ride," he explained. "I'm going to get a fine, juicy bone for Skyrocket."

This took the children's mind off what might have been a sad subject to think about— the ill mother and missing father of Harry and Mary. And when Uncle Toby made Skyrocket sit up in the automobile and "beg" for the bone, the dog did it in such a funny way that the children all laughed.

"Now they'll be all right," said Uncle Toby to himself, as he again sent the big car forward.

Soon they were out in the country. The weather was pleasant after the storm, though it was cold, and would soon be more frosty, for winter was at hand, and the children had already begun to think of Christmas.

As Aunt Sallie had said, there had been placed in the automobile a number of boxes of lunch to be eaten on the way, as it would be night, or very near it, before the cabin in the woods could be reached. Uncle Toby had written to a lumberman to build a fire in it so the place would be warm for the children. It was a large roomy cabin, with many comforts and conveniences. Having the lunch in the automobile, the next thing to think about was the time to eat it.

Possibly the boys thought more about this than the girls; at any rate that must have been the reason why Tom and Ted so often asked Uncle Toby what time it was, for the clock on the instrument board of the automobile was not going.

"Well, it will soon be eating time, if that's what you want to know," answered Uncle Toby, with a laugh, after this same question had been asked many times. He seemed to be always laughing.

"In fact we may as well get the lunch out now, I guess, Aunt Sallie," he went on. "We had an early breakfast and—"

He suddenly stopped talking, for there was a loud hissing sound from beneath the automobile, as if a big snake had had its tail run over.

"Puncture!" cried Tom and Ted, for they knew enough about cars to tell this.

"Well, I'm glad it isn't a blow-out!" Uncle Toby exclaimed. Had there been a blow-out the noise would have been much louder, like the bang of a gun. "As long as it's only a puncture we can easily mend it, and I'll do that while the rest of you eat."

"Oh, let me help!" begged Ted. "I often help daddy when he has tire trouble."

"I want to help, too," cried Tom.

"So do I," added Harry. "We never had an auto," he went on, "so I don't know anything about them. But I'll do what I can."

"Well, you boys can hand me the tools," said Uncle Toby, "and I'll do the hard work. This is a heavy car and I don't want you getting into any danger around it. You can be getting out the lunch, Aunt Sallie. We'll be ready to eat after we finish putting in a new rubber tube."

"We'll help," offered Jan and the other two girls, while Trouble cried:

"I want to see punchure! Want to see punchure!"

"No, you stay in here," said his sister, for she knew he would only get in the way if allowed to run about. "I'll let you open some of the boxes."

This satisfied Trouble, who was now content to stay in the big car. Skyrocket, though, went out with the boys and nosed about in the woods near which the stop had been made.

It did not take Uncle Toby long to jack up the car, take off the tire, put in a new tube, and be ready to start again. But before doing that they halted a bit longer to eat lunch. Hot chocolate had been brought along in thermos bottles, and Uncle Toby thought the chocolate would spill on the children if they tried to drink it while the automobile was moving.

"There! I feel better!" exclaimed Ted, after the lunch.

"So do I!" cried Tom and Harry.

Once more they were on their way, journeying now along some country road, and again through some lonely stretch of wood. They were almost at Crystal Lake, and in another quarter of an hour would be at Uncle Toby's cabin, when Mr. Bardeen began sniffing the air.

"The engine's getting too hot," he said, and then, as he noticed some steam coming out of the radiator cap he added: "Water's getting low. I'll have to stop and get some."

"Where can you get any water around here?" asked Ted.

"I'll try at that cabin," answered Uncle Toby, pointing to a lonely one a short distance ahead on the road. "I guess it will be safe to run the car that much farther."

"Who lives there?" asked Ted, as the automobile went along more slowly, for Uncle Toby did not want to overheat it.

"Nobody lives there now," was the reply. "It's deserted. But there's a well near it, and it's such a deep one I don't believe it will be frozen. I can get some water from the well."

Uncle Toby stopped the car in front of the lonely cabin. He got out a folding canvas pail from the tool-box, and was going toward the cabin when Ted exclaimed:

"I thought you said nobody lived here, Uncle Toby!"

"So I did," was the answer. "No one has lived here for several years."

"Well, look at him!" cried the boy, and he pointed to a man running away over the field from the back door of the lonely cottage.

CHAPTER XIV

AT CRYSTAL LAKE

Uncle Toby was much surprised at what Ted called to his attention. Turning around, as he was going toward the well, Uncle Toby looked to where the Curlytop boy pointed. He saw the form of a man vanishing from sight over the top of a little hill just behind the lonely cabin.

"Hello there!" cried Uncle Toby, in such loud tones that Skyrocket began to bark fiercely. "Hello there! Who are you? What are you doing?"

The man did not stop, turn around, nor answer. Instead he ran into a little clump of trees and was soon lost to sight. With another loud bark Skyrocket took after him.

"Oh, don't let our dog go!" cried Jan. "Make him come back, Uncle Toby. That man might hurt him."

"Just what I think," said Uncle Toby. "Here, Sky!" he called, for sometimes the Curlytops' dog was given that short name. "Here, Sky! Come back. Come back!"

Skyrocket didn't want to. He dearly loved a chase, and this man seemed willing to run. That the man was out of sight made no difference to the dog. Skyrocket loved a game of hide and go seek, and perhaps he thought that was what the stranger was playing.

"Come back here, Sky!" called Uncle Toby.

"Here, Skyrocket! Here!" shouted Ted.

Janet added her voice to that of her brother and Trouble chimed in. Perhaps all these had an effect on the dog, or he might have thought that Uncle Toby would punish him if he did not mind. At any rate, after a few more barks and some growls, looking meanwhile toward the clump of trees into which the man had disappeared, the dog came back, wagging his tail and seeming a bit disappointed.

"Who was that man, Uncle Toby?" asked Janet.

"I don't know," was the answer. "No one has lived in that cabin for years. I guess he is some tramp who didn't have any other place to stay."

"He didn't look like a tramp," observed Tom.

"No, his clothes weren't ragged," added Ted.

"That's so," agreed Uncle Toby. "From the little look I had of him he wasn't very ragged. But then maybe he hasn't been a tramp very long, and it takes quite a while to make one's clothes ragged."

"It doesn't take Trouble long!" laughed Jan. "He can go out with a good new suit on and come back in half an hour with it all full of cuts and holes."

"Oh, well, Trouble is different," said Uncle Toby, with a chuckle.

Uncle Toby stood for a few moments looking toward the woods into which the strange man had run, and then, going to the well, filled the pail with water and put some in the radiator of the automobile. After that Uncle Toby went around to the back of the old cabin.

"Are you going to see if anybody else is there?" asked Jan, while Lola and Mary waited with curiosity for an answer.

"Let me come and help look!" cried Ted.

"So will I!" added Tom.

"If you fellows are going I might as well go, too," said Harry.

"No, you children stay where you are," called Uncle Toby. "I'm just going to take a look around, and then we'll go on to Crystal Lake. Stay where you are!"

Ted, Janet, and the others remained in the automobile, waiting for Uncle Toby to come back. Aunt Sallie was almost ready to doze off in a little sleep when Mr. Bardeen was seen coming around the corner of the cabin. No one was with him, and there was no further sight of the man.

"Was anybody else in there?" asked Ted.

"No one," replied Uncle Toby. "The cabin was empty as far as I could see. I guess the man just stopped in there for shelter, and when he saw us he thought we owned the place and ran out."

"Who does own it?" asked Tom.

"It belongs to a lumberman named Newt Baker," answered Uncle Toby. "He used to stay here in the summer, and sometimes part of the winter. But he went away and since then no one has lived here—except that tramp," he added with a laugh. "Poor man," he went on, "I hope he finds some place to stay this winter. It looks as if it might be a hard one from the early snow we had."

Once more they started off; and a little later, nothing more having happened, they arrived safely at Crystal Lake.

"Oh, what a fine place!" cried Tom Taylor, as he saw the big body of water, on the shore of which was perched Uncle Toby's cottage. The lake was not frozen, except with a "skim" of ice here and there in little coves.

"It would be lovely in summer for picnics," said Lola. Neither she nor her brother had been to Crystal Lake before, but the Curlytops had visited it once or twice with Uncle Toby, though they had almost forgotten.

"Well, here we are, children!" called Uncle Toby, as he stopped the automobile near his "shack" as he often called it. "Now if you'll see that they get safely inside, Aunt Sallie, I'll soon be with you and we'll look after supper and get the beds ready."

"I not goin' to bed now!" cried Trouble. "I not goin' to bed now! I goin' to stay up an' see—an' see—Santa C'aus!" he burst out, after a moment of thought.

"Oh, you little tyke!" laughed Lola, catching him up in her arms. "Santa Claus won't be here for over a month."

"And you don't have to go to bed right away," added Janet.

Out of the auto piled the boys and girls, Skyrocket scrambling ahead of them to smell around and find out what sort of place this was that he had been brought to.

As Aunt Sallie, the Curlytops and their playmates went toward the front door of the cabin, the door was opened and a smiling man looked out.

"Hello, folks!" he called. "I've got it good and warm for you, though it isn't as cold as it was." He was the man Uncle Toby had engaged to start the fires and to have everything in readiness for the coming of the Curlytops.

"Well, we're glad to get here, Jim Nelson," said Aunt Sallie, for she knew the man.

Uncle Toby put the car in the barn and came in with some of the boxes and bundles that had been piled in the automobile—bundles of clothes and things for the children.

"Well, you got here all right, I see," remarked Jim Nelson. "Have any trouble on the way?"

"Not to amount to anything," answered Uncle Toby. "Funny thing, though, down at Newt Baker's cabin. I stopped there to get some water from his deep well. And as I got near the cabin a man ran out and down the hill."

"A man!" exclaimed Mr. Nelson, while the children listened to the talk. "I didn't know anybody was living there."

"There isn't—that is, not living there regularly," said Uncle Toby. "But a man ran out. I took him for a tramp at first, only he wasn't ragged. But after he ran away I went and looked in."

"What did you see?" asked Mr. Nelson, and this the Curlytops and others wished to hear about.

"Well, it looked as if he'd been living there and doing his cooking for some time," went on Uncle Toby. "There were a lot of tin cans and odds and ends of loaves of bread, cracker crumbs, and the like on the table in the kitchen. Looked to me as if this man had been camping out in Newt Baker's shack."

"Very likely," said Mr. Nelson. "I don't like such characters hanging around Crystal Lake. We'll have to keep watch for him. If there are tramps around they may take things. As a matter of fact, food and little comforts of small value have been taken from some of the cottages and camps. Fred Tuller's son Tom wrote to the Pocono paper and made a whale of a story out of it. But from what you say the matter may be of more importance than we thought. At any rate, we'd better look into it."

"We'll keep a lookout, then," said Uncle Toby. "And I'll take another run down to the cabin some day, after I get the Curlytops settled here having fun," and he laughed at the boys and girls so they would not be afraid of the talk of tramps and men who might take things.

Mr. Nelson left a little after this, promising to come over the next day to see how they were.

Then came busy times in Uncle Toby's cabin at Crystal Lake. Aunt Sallie and the three girls got ready the supper, while the boys opened boxes and bundles. Skyrocket ran about here and there, poking his nose into everything, and Trouble was almost as bad, for he, too, wanted to see everything that was going on.

At last, however, things began to get "straightened out," as the Curlytops' mother would have said, and they sat down to a fine supper. Every one had a good appetite, even Skyrocket, who had gnawed clean the bone Uncle Toby got him at the butcher shop.

"Let's play hide and go seek before we go to bed," proposed Jan, as they sat about the open fireplace in the big living room after supper.

"Will it be all right?" asked Mary.

"Will what be all right?" Jan wanted to know.

"I mean won't your uncle be mad if we play in his house?" went on Mary.

"Oh, dear no!" laughed Jan. "That's what he brought us up here for; didn't you, Uncle Toby?"

"Didn't I what, Jan?" he asked, for he had been talking to Aunt Sallie about the beds.

"Didn't you bring us up here so we could have a good time?"

"Of course I did!" exclaimed Mr. Bardeen. "What do you want to do now?"

"Play hide and go seek. May we?"

"Yes, go ahead. Run about as much as you please, but don't get hurt. There isn't any fancy furniture here to break."

This was true, for everything in the cabin at Crystal Lake was heavy and strongly made to stand rough handling. So the children could do no harm racing about the cabin.

Soon a merry game was in progress, even Trouble taking part, though he could hardly be said to play it right. His idea was to hide and keep on yelling for some one to come and find him, his voice easily telling where he was. The only thing to be done in his case was to pretend not to know where he was, even if one saw him. This always made Trouble scream with delight, and he would say, over and over again:

"You couldn't find me, could you?"

And of course they always said they couldn't, though they could if they had wished.

So the game went on, Trouble taking his part in it. Finally came the turn of Mary to "blind," and as she covered her face and began to count slowly, the others tiptoed into the different rooms to hide. The cabin was built on the bungalow style, with a number of rooms on the first floor, and there were many fine hiding places.

Janet went into a room at the far end of the cabin, a room that no one, so far during the evening, had entered. It was where Uncle Toby was going to sleep.

"No one will find me here," thought Janet, as she crouched down behind a chair near one of the windows. She looked through the glass, and dimly saw the dark forest all around the cabin. "No one will think of coming here," said Janet to herself.

She cuddled herself into as small a nook as possible down behind the chair, in a place where she could look out through the other rooms and could see the lamplight and firelight in the big living apartment.

It was in this living apartment that Mary was counting with her eyes shut and soon she would call: "Ready or not I'm coming!" Then she would walk around and try to find the hiding ones.

"But she won't find me," thought Janet, "and I can get in home free."

From the distance Janet heard Mary say she was coming, and then suddenly the little girl was startled by a tapping on the window just back of the chair behind which she was hiding.

At first Janet thought it was the brushing of some tree branch against the glass that had made the tapping sound. But when it came again, several times, and very regular, the little girl knew some hand must be doing it.

"Maybe Tom or Ted has gone outside and is trying to scare me," thought Janet. "I'll take a peep and see."

Slowly she raised herself up from her crouching position behind the chair. And then the tapping sound on the glass came again. Janet looked out and gave a scream as, looking in through the window, she saw the face of a man on which the moon faintly shone.

CHAPTER XV

ON THE SLIPPERY HILL

Janet Martin had only a glimpse of the face of the man looking in through the window at her after he had tapped on the glass. As soon as he saw some one peering out at him, and as soon as he heard Janet scream—as he must have heard—the man sprang away.

He was soon lost to sight in the woods around the cabin. The moon shone faintly—had it not been for this Jan would never have seen the man's face—but it was not bright enough in the forest to see him after he leaped away from the cabin.

"Oh! Oh! Oh!" screamed Janet. Her voice rang out in the empty room and was heard by Uncle Toby, Aunt Sallie and the children playing hide and go seek.

"What's the matter? What's the matter?" asked Uncle Toby, who was putting wood in the fireplace.

"Oh, it's a man! A man!" cried Janet, running out from Uncle Toby's bedroom into the living apartment where they were now all gathered. "A man looked in the window at me and he tapped on the glass!"

"Who was he?" asked Uncle Toby, grasping a heavy stick of wood. Tom, Ted and Harry at once began to think they had better take some sticks, too, in case there might be a fight. "Was it Jim Nelson?" went on Uncle Toby. "Sometimes he taps on my window when he comes around by the side path."

"I—I couldn't see who it was—except that he was a man," stammered Janet. "As soon as he saw me looking at him he ran away."

"Jim Nelson wouldn't do that unless he was playing a trick," decided Uncle Toby. "And Jim isn't that kind of a man. He wouldn't scare children. I must see who this is!"

"Maybe he's the tramp we saw over at the place where you got the pail of water this afternoon," said Ted.

"Maybe," agreed Uncle Toby. "Well, if he's a poor man and in trouble I'm sorry for him. But he hasn't any right to come sneaking around my cabin, tapping on the window. I'll see about this!"

Uncle Toby went outside, and the boys followed. Trouble wanted to go with Ted, but Janet held back her little brother.

In the moonlight, which was brighter now, as the clouds had blown away, Uncle Toby made a trip around the cabin, taking Skyrocket with him, while the boys, each with a chunk of wood as a weapon, followed Mr. Bardeen.

Uncle Toby called loudly to know who was in the woods, and the dog barked, but no man answered.

"I can't find any one," Uncle Toby announced, coming back into the cabin with the boys. "It's too dark to see if there are any strange footprints in the snow, and I don't believe we could tell by them anyhow, as Jim Nelson and some of his friends have been tramping around here the last few days, bringing in wood and things. Are you sure you saw a man at the window, Janet?"

"Sure, Uncle Toby. And I heard him tapping on the glass, too."

"Well, I don't believe he meant any harm. Maybe he was the tramp we saw at the lonely cabin, or it may have been another. He may have wanted shelter for the night, and something to eat. But when he heard you scream it must have frightened him off, as he may have had an idea he'd be scolded for frightening a little girl. Anyhow, no harm is done, and there will be no danger. Go on with your game."

However, the children were too excited over what had happened to do this. Janet was trembling, and the others wanted her to tell over again just what had happened. And as Janet told and retold it she became less frightened, until finally she was laughing as though it had been a joke.

"But if I'd 'a' got that man I'd 'a' hit him with a stick of wood!" threatened Ted.

"So would I!" declared Tom and Harry.

"Perhaps it's just as well you didn't find him then," said Uncle Toby, with a laugh.

After the children had gone to bed—and Uncle Toby said the look of them all tucked in made him think of a boarding school—he and Aunt Sallie sat up a bit longer.

"Do you really think Janet saw a man?" asked Aunt Sallie. "And if so, who was he?"

"That's more than I can tell," Uncle Toby answered. "Janet isn't the kind of girl to imagine things. I believe it was a man. Probably the same fellow we saw running away from the lonely cabin. To-morrow I'll take Jim Nelson and some of the men

93 | P a g e

and we'll have a look around. I don't want rough and strange men roaming these woods when I have a lot of children out here for the holidays."

"I should say not!" exclaimed Aunt Sallie. "I wouldn't like it myself! And maybe he's the man who's been taking things."

"Maybe," agreed Uncle Toby.

However, there were no more alarms nor any trouble that night, and after a few minutes of lying awake Janet went to sleep as soundly as the other children. They slept rather late the next morning, for they were tired with the travel of the day before, and when Jan and Lola came down to the kitchen they found Aunt Sallie getting breakfast.

"Oh, we said we'd get up and help!" exclaimed Jan. For she had promised her mother, on leaving home to visit Uncle Toby and Aunt Sallie, that she would help with the housework.

"And I used to get breakfast all alone," said Mary. "That is after mother was sick," and she could not keep back a few tears, though she turned her head away so the other girls would not see them.

"Never mind, my dear," said Aunt Sallie, with a laugh. "I didn't want you to get up early. Uncle Toby told me to let you girls and the boys sleep."

"Oh, aren't the boys up yet?" asked Jan, with a laugh.

"Don't tell me we've beaten!" added Lola, with a giggle.

"They said they were going to get up and see the sun rise," remarked Mary.

"I guess they forgot it, or else they thought they could see the sun some other morning," laughed Aunt Sallie. "For they aren't down yet, though it's almost time to call them, for I'm going to start to bake the pancakes soon."

"Oh, are you going to have pancakes?" cried Jan.

"Yes, and with maple syrup," Aunt Sallie answered.

"Oh, I love them!" exclaimed Lola. "Don't you, Mary?"

"I—I don't know," was the hesitating answer. "I—I guess I never had any."

"Oh my, just—" but Lola stopped. She was going to say "just fancy a girl never having eaten pancakes with maple syrup!" But she thought it would not be polite to say that, so she changed it to:

"Just you wait until you try them! You'll love them!"

"I know Ted does, so I'm going to call him!" exclaimed Janet. "He wouldn't want to keep on sleeping and miss the cakes."

"Tom wouldn't, either," declared Lola.

So they called the boys, who soon rushed downstairs, as hungry as ever any boys were. And the girls were quite as hungry. As for Trouble, he always thought he was hungry whether he was or not.

Uncle Toby came in, having been out to do the chores, he said. He had also been over to Jim Nelson's cabin to talk about the man who had tapped on the window, scaring Janet. But Uncle Toby said nothing about this. Instead he said:

"Getting colder, boys and girls. Hope you brought your skates."

"Why," asked Ted, "is there skating?"

"No; but there will be. Shouldn't wonder but what part of the lake would freeze over by to-morrow. But don't any of you go on until I try the ice to see if it's safe."

"Guess there isn't any danger of me going on," remarked Harry Benton.

"Why not?" asked Ted. "Don't you like to skate?"

"Sure I do!" Harry answered. "But I haven't any skates."

"I brought some extra pairs along," remarked Uncle Toby. "I think I have some that will fit you and Mary."

"Oh, goodie!" cried Mary, for she felt she could now have fun like the other girls.

"But it hasn't frozen yet, though it soon will be," said Uncle Toby. "Well, I'm going to leave you youngsters to amuse yourselves for a while, as I have some things to look after."

Uncle Toby paused for a moment and then went on.

"Now about school."

"Yes," said Ted, in a low voice. "I s'pose we'll have to go," he added, with a sigh.

"No!" exclaimed Uncle Toby. "That's the queer part of it. You can't go. I told your folks you could, but you can't."

"Why not?" asked Jan, and neither she nor any of the others seemed disappointed.

"The teacher they had here was taken sick, I've just heard, and they can't get another until after the holidays. So it doesn't look as though you could go to school. I'm sorry—"

"Oh, ho!" cried the Curlytops and their playmates. "No school! Hurray!"

"Now we'll go out and have some fun!" shouted Ted, as Uncle Toby left the cabin.

"Me come!" cried Trouble.

"Yes, we'll take you," answered Lola.

"Take good care of Trouble!" called Aunt Sallie to the boys and girls as they started from the cabin. They were warmly dressed, as it was getting colder, just as Uncle Toby had declared.

"We'll watch him!" called back Jan.

Off through the trees, under which, here and there, were patches of snow, wandered the Curlytops and their playmates. They laughed and shouted, running here and there until they were nearly as warm as on a summer's day. It was sheltered under the trees, but out in the open was getting colder, and in places thin ice was forming on Crystal Lake.

They walked along, sometimes all together and again with the boys running ahead of the girls, until they came to a little hill, covered with pine trees. The wind had swept the ground bare of snow here, or else it had melted, and in places were patches of the long, smooth and slippery pine needles.

Tom, Ted, and Harry had run off to one side, for Skyrocket had scared up a rabbit and the boys wanted to see the bunny, though they would not have let the dog harm it. Trouble started to follow his brother and the other two lads, but as he reached the top of the pine-needle-covered hill Janet called him back.

"Trouble, come here!" she exclaimed.

"No!" he answered. "I go see bunny rabbit!"

"No, you must stay with me," said Janet, starting after him. Trouble gathered himself to spring away on a run, but suddenly there was a queer screeching call in a tree over his head, and a moment later the little fellow went sliding and slipping down the hill and out of sight.

"Oh, dear!" cried Janet

"Was it an eagle that screamed?" asked Lola, who did not know much about birds.

"Maybe the eagle carried him off," suggested Mary, who knew even less about the creatures of the woods.

"There aren't any eagles around here, I hope," said Janet. "But something happened to Trouble! I hope he isn't hurt!"

Again came that shrill, harsh call. It sounded like:

"Hay! Hay! Hay!"

"Somebody is laughing because Trouble fell downhill," said Lola. "I wonder if it's that horrid old man?"

A moment later there was a rustling in the bushes, and a large bird with bright blue feathers marked with patches of white flew up into a tree harshly crying:

"Hay! Hay! Hay!"

"Oh, it's a blue jay!" exclaimed Janet, as she ran to the top of the hill to see what had happened to William. It was nothing serious. He had merely slid down on the smooth brown pine needles which covered the ground and made it almost as slippery as a coasting hill. Perhaps the sudden cry of the blue jay had made Trouble give a nervous jump and this had thrown him off his balance, causing him to fall.

"Was that bird chase me?" he asked, as he heard the blue one cry and saw it flitting about.

"Oh, no," answered Lola. "You chased yourself, I guess. Are you hurt?"

"I—I'm all—bumped," explained Trouble.

And this, really, was all that had happened to him. The pine hill was so smooth that no one could have been hurt on it. The girls found it so slippery that they could hardly stand up on it while helping Trouble up.

"Let's try—" began Mary. She was about to say "try a slide," when her feet suddenly went from under her and she did as Trouble had done. She burst out laughing, as did William and the other two girls, and the woods echoed to the merry sound, bringing the boys over on the run. They had not seen the rabbit after the first fleeting glimpse.

"What's the matter?" asked Ted.

"We've found a slippery place," answered his sister.

"Come on, let's try it!" suggested Tom.

They all did, making efforts to go down the slippery pine-needle hill standing up. But every one toppled before reaching the bottom of the hill. However, this was part of the fun, and Trouble enjoyed it with the others.

Now and then the blue jay would flit to and fro, alighting on the trees or bushes, and shrilly cry:

"Hay! Hay! Hay!"

"Maybe he wants to play, too," suggested Mary, who liked to look at one of our most brilliantly colored winter birds.

"He's making enough fuss about it, anyhow," said Tom.

The children had lots of fun in the woods that day and the next. No more tappings on the window were heard, and the Curlytops and their playmates forgot all about the little scare. The weather grew colder and colder. One morning Uncle Toby came in from the barn. He rubbed his red hands before the fire and said:

"Lake's frozen over! Now you can go skating!"

CHAPTER XVI

A REAL TOBOGGAN

"Let's have a race!" cried Ted, as soon as his skates were fastened on his shoes, for as soon as breakfast was over the children had gone out on the ice with their skates.

"All right!" shouted Tom, who was quite ready for this sort of fun. "I can beat you, Ted Martin!"

"And I can beat you, Tom Taylor!" exclaimed Lola, his sister, who was a very good skater.

"Oh, wouldn't it be fun if we two could beat them?" suggested Jan to Lola.

"We'll try," was the answer.

Meanwhile, though Mary and Harry had put on their skates, they took no part in this talk and stood about on the ice as if they hardly knew what to do.

"Will you join in the race?" asked Lola of Mary. "We three girls against the boys."

"I don't believe I can skate well enough to race," Mary answered, and her brother joined in with:

"You see we never had much chance to skate, and about all we can do is to move along in a straight line." He laughed good-naturedly over his own lack of skill.

"Oh, that's all right!" cried Ted, in jolly fashion. "We won't have any race then—that is, until after you two get more used to your skates."

"Oh, don't let us stop you from having fun!" exclaimed Mary.

"We can have just as much fun not racing. I don't care much for it, anyhow, do you, Jan?" said Lola.

"No, indeed!" answered the Curlytop girl. Thus did they try to make Mary and Harry feel happier, and they succeeded.

"I tell you what we can do," suggested Tom Taylor. "Ted and I can show you a few easy tricks on skates, Harry, and Jan and Lola can do the same with Mary."

"That will be fine!" exclaimed Harry. "Then, when we know more about it, we can have a race."

So it was decided, and then and there began lessons for the two poor children whom Uncle Toby had brought to Crystal Lake so they might have a good time over the holidays. Harry and Mary were quick to learn, and though it would be some time before they could beat any of the other four children in a race, they did very well for beginners.

"See if you can do this!" cried Ted, after having shown Harry how to "grind the bar" backward, a trick Harry soon learned.

"Watch me!" cried Ted, as he began doing what he called a grapevine twist. To do it he darted farther out from shore than any of them had yet gone, and just as he was dong some fancy skating there was a loud booming, cracking sound that sent a shiver all through the ice on which the others were standing.

"Oh, come! Come back!" cried Jan to her brother. "The ice is going to break! We'll fall in!"

"That's right!" yelled Tom. "Come on back, Ted!"

Ted needed no urging, but skated as fast as he could toward shore, whither the others were fleeing as fast as they could strike out on their skates. They reached land safely, and, to their surprise, no big cracks or holes appeared in the ice. It seemed as solid as ever.

"I wonder what made that?" asked Janet, whose heart was beating fast.

"The ice broke somewhere," declared Lola.

"We'd better not go on it any more," said Mary.

"Well go up and ask Uncle Toby about it," suggested Ted. "I don't want to stop skating."

As the children were about to take off their skates to go back to the cabin, Aunt Sallie was seen coming down, dragging Trouble on a sled. There were patches of snow here and there so it was not hard to pull the sled along. And Trouble was not very heavy.

"Oh, Aunt Sallie, you ought to hear the ice crack!" called the children in a chorus.

"Is it dangerous?" asked Mary.

Uncle Toby came out of the bungalow and heard what was asked.

"That rumbling, cracking sound isn't anything dangerous," he said. "The ice often does that, and often big cracks come in it out in the middle of the lake. But it is thick enough, and it won't break through with you or I shouldn't have let you go skating. But, even with all I have said, don't go too far out."

The children felt safer, now that Uncle Toby had told them this, and Ted again started to show Harry how to do a grapevine twist. Aunt Sallie gave the sled and Trouble over in charge of the girls, and they skated up and down pulling William to and fro, to his great delight.

The boys, now that Harry felt more at home on his skates, began to try to outdo each other in tricks, and when Harry said he would be the judge, Tom and Ted had a race, Ted winning.

Once Jan and Lola skated so fast, pretending they were a team of horses pulling Trouble on his sled, that Jan stumbled and fell down, also tripping Lola. The girls were not hurt, and they slid along over the ice laughing. But the sled was upset, Trouble fell off, and though he was so bundled up that he didn't get hurt, he began to cry.

"I guess we'd better take him in," suggested Jan. "He may be cold. Anyhow, I've had enough skating."

"So have I," said Mary and Lola.

They went up to the cabin, taking Trouble with them. But the boys remained on the ice a while longer, and Harry was rapidly becoming a good skater.

The three lads did not take off their skates until it was time for dinner, and after the meal they went back on the frozen lake again, though the girls stayed in to play with their dolls.

"Make the most of your skating," said Uncle Toby, as he watched the three lads circling around on the ice.

"Why?" asked Tom.

"Because I think we are going to have another storm," was the answer. "It is going to snow, and then all the ice will be covered. Of course you can scrape clean a small place, but it will be hard work. So get all the skating you can while it's good."

This the boys did, that day and the next. But the following morning, when they awakened and looked from the windows, they saw the ground white with snow, and more flakes coming down.

"Hurray!" cried Tom. "Now we can have fun coasting!"

"And maybe we can make a toboggan slide!" added Ted.

"I've seen them," remarked Harry, "but I was never on one."

"We had a wooden one in our yard, but we had to put candle grease on our sled runners first," Ted explained. "It would be great if we could make a regular toboggan slide."

"Let's ask Uncle Toby," suggested Janet.

Uncle Toby laughed in jolly fashion as the Curlytops and their playmates swarmed around him in the cozy cabin.

"A toboggan slide, eh?" he cried. "Well, I don't see why you can't have one, and you don't need to build it of wood, either, for there's a good hill not far away. But how would you like to coast on a regular toboggan instead of your sleds?"

"Oh, could we?" shouted Ted.

"I guess so," was the answer. "There's a French Canadian who lives not far away, and he has a big toboggan. We'll go over in the auto and see if he'll let us take it. I used to have one out here, but I find that it's broken."

"Oh, what fun we'll have!" sang Janet, and the others joined in the chorus of joy.

It kept on snowing, but they could journey out in the big, closed automobile even with the storm all about, and this they soon did.

"But if we get the toboggan how can we get it in here? There isn't much room," remarked Ted, for the children and Uncle Toby almost filled the big machine.

"Oh, we'll tie it on behind and pull it over," said Uncle Toby. "A toboggan can go faster than any auto."

"I ride on it!" said Trouble, and the others laughed, for of course he didn't know what he was talking about.

The road to the cabin of the French Canadian lumberman who owned the big toboggan ran past the lonely shack where Uncle Toby had once stopped for water and from which the strange man had run away. As they neared this cabin again Ted asked:

"I wonder if that man is in there now?"

"I don't know," said Uncle Toby. "But I think I'll take a look. Jim Nelson and I meant to do it before this, but we haven't had a chance. We don't want any tramps living in our woods."

He stopped the machine near the cabin and got out. The boys wanted to follow him, but he told them to remain with the girls.

"I'm just going to look in the window," said Uncle Toby.

He did this, first at the front windows, and evidently saw nothing, for he soon went around to the rear. And suddenly the children in the automobile heard shouting, and the shouts came from inside the cabin.

"Somebody's there!" cried Ted, starting to get out.

"You stay here!" cried Janet, catching her brother by the coat. "Uncle Toby told you to stay here!"

As Ted sank back in his seat they could all hear Uncle Toby saying:

"Who are you? What are you doing in there?"

The man in the lonely cabin answered, but what he said the Curlytops and their playmates could not tell. There was more shouting to and fro between Uncle Toby and the unknown man, and then Mr. Bardeen came around to the front of the cabin.

"Is he there? Who is he? What does he want?" The children quickly asked these questions.

"Oh, he's just a tramp I guess," answered Uncle Toby. "I couldn't make much out of him. But I'll tell Jim Nelson and some of the lumbermen, and we'll see what he's doing there. He can't do much harm, for there isn't anything of value in the old shack. But it's just as well not to have a tramp in there."

Once again Uncle Toby started the machine, and soon they were at the cabin of the French Canadian.

"Could we borrow your toboggan, Jules?" asked Uncle Toby.

"Oh, of a sure yes!" was the answer, Jules doing his best to speak what to him was a new language. "I bring she out to you!"

He ran around to the back of his shack, and soon came into view again with a real toboggan, at the sight of which the children set up a joyous shout.

CHAPTER XVII

THE SNOW HOUSE

The Frenchman's toboggan was a large one. It would hold all of the Curlytops and their playmates, with room to spare. I suppose most of you have seen toboggans, or pictures of them, and know what they are. Instead of being made like a sled, with steel runners, a toboggan is like a thin, flat board, with the front end curled up like the old fashioned Dutch skates. Only instead of being made of one flat piece of wood, a large toboggan is made of several strips fastened together so it will not so easily break.

On the side of Jules's toboggan were hand rails, to which the riders could hold. There was also a cushion on which to sit, and altogether it was a very fine way of coasting downhill.

"Oh, what fun we'll have on this!" cried Jan.

"Will it go fast?" asked Lola.

"It'll go like an express train!" cried Ted.

"And we fellows will take turns sitting on the back and sticking our feet out to steer," added Tom, for that is how a toboggan is guided, you know.

"If it's going as fast as an express train I don't believe I want to ride," said Mary, who was rather more timid than the other children.

"Don't let those boys scare you," advised Janet. "They're only talking to hear themselves talk. Tom and Ted are always that way—aren't they, Lola?"

"Yes," answered Tom's sister, with a laugh.

The boys were now clustered around the big toboggan, and Trouble had taken his seat in the middle of the cushion.

"You give me wide!" he demanded of his brother.

"Not now a little later," promised Ted. He wanted to listen to what the Canadian was saying, telling Uncle Toby how the big toboggan was best managed on a hill.

"I'll go down with the children the first few times," said Uncle Toby, "to make sure it's all right. Our hill isn't so very steep, and I don't believe there's much danger."

"On little hill not—no!" exclaimed Jules, with a smile that showed all his white teeth. "But on big hill, steep so like roof of house, toboggan her go like what you say—fifty-nine?"

"I guess you mean like sixty," laughed Uncle Toby.

"Mebby so. Her go very fast. I like for childrens to have good time, but not too fast!"

"I'll see that they are careful," promised Uncle Toby.

After much teasing the three boys were allowed to sit on the toboggan after it was tied to the rear of the automobile for the trip home.

"I won't go very fast," said Uncle Toby. "But if I should have to stop you boys will need to stick your feet down in the snow suddenly to put on the brakes, you know, or you'll bump into my rear wheels."

"We'll do that," promised Tom, Ted, and Harry.

Trouble wanted to ride with the boys on the toboggan as it was drawn along over the snow behind the auto, but he was not allowed to do this, as it was thought his brother and the other two lads would be so full of fun that they would forget to watch him, and he might fall off and be left behind.

The toboggan was made fast with a long rope, the boys took their places, and with many thanks to Jules for his kindness, the trip home was begun.

"Hurray!" cried Ted. "Here we go!"

"Talk about fun!" shouted Tom. "We're having it all right!"

"I never had such a good time in my life," said Harry, his eyes shining with pleasure. He wished his mother might have shared in some of his and his sister's enjoyment, and how he wished that he had a father, such as the other boys had, only he himself knew. But he said nothing of this.

"Hold on tightly now, boys!" called Uncle Toby.

"We will!" they answered, and away they went.

At first everything was all right. The road was slightly uphill and the toboggan kept well back from the wheels of the automobile, so there was no danger of bumping into them. But when the automobile started down grade toward Uncle Toby's cabin, the wooden sled slid faster than the automobile was pulling it.

"Put on brakes! Put on brakes!" shouted Ted.

"Stick your feet in the snow!" echoed Tom.

The three boys thrust their feet out on either side of the toboggan, digging their heels into the snow, and in this way they made themselves slow up, so they did not hit the wheels. Even if they had done so no harm would have resulted, because the wheels had large rubber tires on them, and the front of the toboggan came up in a big curve.

Soon they were going uphill again, and the boys did not have to "put on brakes." But as Uncle Toby made the automobile go a bit faster, when they were near his cabin, he and the girls suddenly heard laughing shouts from the boys behind them.

"Oh, something has happened!" exclaimed Jan, looking out of the rear window of the closed car.

"They've fallen off!" added Mary. "I hope they aren't hurt!"

"Can't be much hurt, falling off in the snow," laughed Uncle Toby, as he brought the car to a stop, got out, and went back, followed by the girls. The toboggan had turned upside down, but was not damaged. The boys, laughing so joyously that they could hardly walk, were coming along, covered with snow.

"What happened?" Uncle Toby wanted to know.

"Oh, the toboggan struck a big lump of snow in the middle of the road and turned right over. It spilled us off!" explained Ted.

"But it was fun!" added Harry. And so it was.

"Well, we're almost there. Better walk the rest of the way," advised Uncle Toby. "Take the toboggan off and pull it."

This was done, two of the boys taking turns pulling the third over the short distance remaining.

"And now for some real tobogganing!" cried Ted, as the cabin was reached.

Uncle Toby, however, would not let the children go down alone for the first few times. He wanted to be sure the boys knew how to manage the big sled, which, though large, was very light, as all toboggans are, and thus are much safer than a sled with steel runners.

There was a long, but not too steep, hill near the cabin, and the Curlytops and their playmates were soon at the top of this, with Uncle Toby and the toboggan.

"All aboard!" called Mr. Bardeen, and they took their places on the cushion, holding to the hand rails. Trouble was not allowed to go down the first time, but Aunt Sallie had all she could do to keep him with her as she stood at the top of the slope watching the coasting party.

"You shall soon have a ride, Trouble," Aunt Sallie promised. "As soon as the hill is made a little smooth."

"All ready?" cried Uncle Toby.

"Let's go!" cried Ted.

Uncle Toby gave a push with his foot, which he had thrust out behind to steer with, and down the snow-covered hill went the toboggan with its happy load. They did not go very fast on this first trip, as the snow needed to be packed down smooth and hard. But after the second or third voyage the toboggan moved more swiftly.

"Do you like it Mary?" asked Janet.

"Oh, I just love it!" cried the other, with shining eyes.

Uncle Toby, finding that everything was safe, allowed the boys, one after another, to try steering the light, wooden sled. Finding that they could manage all right, he let them have charge of the toboggan, and at last Trouble was allowed to coast down, sitting between Lola and Janet.

Of course Trouble wanted to take his turn at steering with the other boys, but that was out of the question, even though he teased very much. It would not have been safe, of course.

And such fun as the Curlytops and their playmates had! The toboggan was much better than a sled, and safer, even though it went faster. It was almost like flying with the snowbirds, Lola said.

Of course there were little accidents and upsets. Once, when Harry was steering, the toboggan turned completely around when half way down the hill and began sliding backward. And as the back end was blunt, having no curve to slip easily over the snow, there was a turnover, and the children were spilled all the way down the hill.

But they never minded that, only rolling over and over to the bottom, or nearly there, laughing and shouting meanwhile. It was fun for Skyrocket, too, the dog leaping here and there, barking and chasing snowballs which the girls threw for him to race after.

Once they took Skyrocket down on the toboggan with them, or, rather, they took him half way, for midway on the hill Skyrocket decided he didn't like that way of traveling, and with a howl he leaped off. It was too swift for him, I suppose.

But the children had great delight in it, and would have kept on with the toboggan fun all day if Uncle Toby had let them. He did not want them to get too tired, however, nor did Aunt Sallie want Trouble to stay out in the cold too long, though he was a sturdy little chap.

After lunch, when Trouble was having his usual nap, Lola and Jan said they would like to try steering the toboggan, and Uncle Toby said they might.

"Well, we fellows won't ride if you girls steer," declared Ted. "You'd upset us first shot."

"Pooh! You don't need to ride!" laughed Janet. "We can do better without you."

The girls learned to steer, after a lesson or two from Uncle Toby. Even timid Mary managed to do quite well, though Janet and Lola, being more used to outdoor life in the country, did better than Mary. The girls had their little accidents, too, upsetting more than once, but they did not mind this.

For several days, while the snow lasted, the Curlytops and their friends had fun in the snow. The weather was bright and sunny, and not too cold. One day Janet, going out to the kitchen where Aunt Sallie was busy, found the table covered with packages and bundles that Uncle Toby had brought from the village store.

"What's going on?" asked Janet.

"Thanksgiving will soon be going on," answered Aunt Sallie. "I must get my mincemeat made, and do a lot of planning for the big family I expect to have at dinner."

"Oh, I didn't know Thanksgiving was so near!" exclaimed Janet. At first she was joyous, and then a little feeling of sadness came to her. This would be the first Thanksgiving she remembered when daddy and mother were not present. The other children, too, when they were told about the coming feast at Uncle Toby's cabin, looked a little serious when they realized that none of their grown-ups would be with them. Of course Mary and Harry did not expect this, for they knew their mother could not come from the hospital for a long time, and as for their father—they had given him up as dead, long ago.

"But maybe daddy and mother will be here for Christmas!" said Janet.

"Maybe!" agreed Ted.

"I'm going to write and ask our father and mother to come here for Christmas. May I, Uncle Toby?" asked Lola, for in common with the Curlytops she called Mr. Bardeen by this name.

"Of course!" Uncle Toby answered. "The more the merrier! And if your mother is able to come from the hospital, we'll have her here for Christmas," and he nodded at Mary and Harry. This made that boy and girl very happy, for it is often happiness just to think of something pleasant that may happen.

One morning, several days after the first of the toboggan riding, the boys, who had gotten up ahead of the girls for once, began shouting outside the cabin.

"What's going on, I wonder?" asked Janet.

"Oh, I guess they're just yelling for the fun of it," answered Lola.

"They're saying something about a house," said Mary.

Janet raised the window and listened. Just then Ted shouted:

"Come on out, girls, and help us build a snow house. We're going to make the biggest snow house you ever saw!"

"And when it's finished you can have a tea party in it," added Tom.

"Oh, what lovely fun that will be!" cried Mary.

Soon the boys and girls, with Skyrocket frolicking around them, began making the snow house. The sun had so warmed the snow that it packed well.

First a number of big snowballs were rolled and placed one after the other in the form of a square on the ground. This was to be the foundation of the house.

Other snowballs were lifted on top of the first large ones, and snow packed in the cracks until, when afternoon came, there were four walls of snow, much higher than the heads of the children.

"It looks more like a fort than a snow house," said Lola.

"We've got to put the roof on," Tom answered. "How we going to do that, Ted?"

"I don't know," was the reply. "I never made such a big snow house. If we make the roof only of snow it will fall in on us."

"You'd better ask Uncle Toby," suggested Janet, and this they did.

"I'll show you how to make a good roof," Uncle Toby told the children. "Just get me a lot of poles from that pile over there. I used them to raise beans this summer. Bring me a lot of those long poles."

The children ran to carry them to him, wondering how Uncle Toby could make a roof on a snow house out of poles.

OTHER SNOWBALLS WERE LIFTED ON TOP OF THE FIRST LARGE
ONES.

CHAPTER XVIII

THANKSGIVING

Perhaps if the Curlytops and their playmates had thought about it a little harder they might have guessed how Uncle Toby intended to make the roof of their snow house with the bean poles. It was very simple.

When the boys and girls had brought a number of the long, thin poles to him, Uncle Toby took the poles, one at a time, and laid them carefully across the tops of the white walls. Each end of the pole rested on the wall, and when all were in place, laid close together, there was the beginning of the roof.

"But it's full of holes," objected Ted, as he went in through the doorway that had been left, and, looking up, could see the sky in between the spaces of the poles.

"Yes, of course it's full of holes," laughed Uncle Toby. "All you have to do is to plaster some snow in the cracks, and then cover the poles with more snow and you'll have a roof to your house that won't fall in on you."

"Why, how easy!" cried Tom. "It's a wonder we didn't think of that ourselves."

"You'll know how next time," replied Uncle Toby. "Bring a few more poles."

This the children did, even Trouble dragging over some of the smallest ones from the pile. Then the roof was ready for its coating of snow, and the children began tossing it on with their hands and from shovels.

At first the snow dropped through some of the larger cracks between the poles, but these were soon filled, and then a solid mass of white was spread over the roof of the snow house.

"I'm going to see if I can't plaster some snow over the poles from inside, so they won't show," decided Ted, when the outside top of the roof was finished. "Then it will look like a solid snow roof."

The other boys helped with this, but it was not as easy as they had thought it would be. For often after they had stuck a handful of snow on the ceiling inside, it would fall down, once or twice right in their faces.

But at last they had the inside poles pretty well plastered over with snow, and the house was finished. There was a doorway, and two windows, and over the door a blanket was hung. Uncle Toby put some sheets of ice in the windows, and they looked just like glass.

"Oh, this is the nicest snow house I ever saw!" cried Janet.

"It's like a fairy one!" exclaimed Mary. "I never dreamed of one so nice as this."

"It's the best one we ever made," said Ted, and the other boys agreed with him.

But the fun was only beginning. The girls had been promised, if they helped with the making of the snow house, that they could have a play party in it for themselves and, if they chose, their dolls.

"We'll ask Aunt Sallie for something to eat and have the play party now," decided Janet, when some boxes had been put in the snow house to serve as tables and chairs.

"Will the dolls eat everything?" asked Tom, with a smile.

"What do you mean—eat everything?" his sister wanted to know.

"I mean will there be anything left for us?" and Tom winked at the other boys.

"Oh, I guess Aunt Sallie will give enough for everybody," said Janet, and Aunt Sallie did.

As she was getting ready for Thanksgiving, there was plenty to eat in Uncle Toby's bungalow, and soon sandwiches and cake, and a tin pail full of hot chocolate were carried out to the snow house.

"It's a regular picnic in the snow!" cried Mary, in delight. "I never knew anything as nice as this."

The girls took their dolls out to the snow house, Mary having brought hers from home with her, and though it was not as well dressed or as costly as the dolls of Janet or Lola, still Mary loved her "child" just as much.

Janet wanted to make Trouble a rag doll to play with, but he insisted that he was an "Indian," for that is what the other boys were pretending to be.

"An' Injuns don't have dolls!" declared Trouble, as he sat on a box in the snow house and sipped his warm chocolate.

For two or three days the children played in the snow house, the weather being mild, so that it was quite comfortable in the white "igloo," as Uncle Toby called it. The children wanted to know where that name came from, and he told them it was what the Eskimos of the Polar regions called their egg-shape huts of ice and snow.

The pole roof was a great success, for it did not fall in on the heads of the boys and girls. And there is nothing worse, when you are having fun in a snow house, than to have the roof cave in on you.

Of course there were little accidents, caused by the snow which the boys had plastered to the inside of the poles. More than once little chunks of snow fell, but they were so light they did no harm, even when they hit Janet or Lola on the head.

Once, however, just as Ted was lifting a cup of chocolate to his mouth, a chunk of snow fell right into the cup, splashing the chocolate all over the lad. Luckily it was not hot, though after the splashing was over Ted looked as if he had colored himself to take part in a minstrel show.

The other children laughed, and so did Ted, after his first surprise.

"To-morrow will be Thanksgiving!" exclaimed Lola one night, as they hurried in from a long day of fun.

"And you ought to see the big pile of good things there are to eat!" exclaimed Tom. "Oh, boys!"

"Aunt Sallie sure has cooked a lot!" cried Ted.

"The most I ever saw," added Harry. "And such a turkey!"

"And such cranberry sauce!" sighed his sister.

"An' there's candy an' nuts an'—an' lots of things!" added Trouble. "It's mos' like Ch'is'mus!"

"Yes, it surely is," agreed Janet. "Only I hope by Christmas we'll have daddy and mother here." A letter had come from Mr. and Mrs. Martin from the distant city where they had gone to see about the money. In the letter the parents of the Curlytops said they hoped to be with them at Christmas.

The father and mother of Tom and Lola had also written, wishing the children the joys of a happy Thanksgiving, and saying they would come up at Christmas with Mr. and Mrs. Martin.

There was also a letter from Mrs. Benton, in which the poor woman said that she had been operated on, and was much better, but added that she would have to be under the doctor's care and in the hospital some time yet.

"Anyhow, it's something to be thankful for," said Mary. Her brother agreed with her. And if in their hearts there was a little sadness because they had no father to share the joys of the holidays with them, they kept it to themselves.

"We all have lots to be thankful for," said Aunt Sallie, when the feast day came. "Yes, and you shall have something, too," she added to Skyrocket, who was sniffing hungrily at the kitchen door.

After breakfast Uncle Toby took them all to the village church in the automobile, though of course Skyrocket was left at the cabin. He did not like it very much, either, and howled dismally after the Curlytops.

Home they drove, through the crisp air of the woods, to take part in the bountiful feast that was ready all but the "finishing touches," as Aunt Sallie called them.

And such a feast as it was! Never was there such a browned turkey! Never such jolly red mounds of cranberry sauce, almost like jelly! Never such crisp celery! And the gravy that covered the heaping plates that the children had passed to them! Surely never was such gravy made!

"Oh, I don't believe I can ever eat another thing!" exclaimed Mary, when Uncle Toby asked her to have another slice of turkey.

"Hasn't you got any room left?" asked Trouble, patting his own little stomach. "I got some room. I saved it for the *ice-cream*!" he added, hoarsely whispering the last word.

"Oh, is there ice-cream?" asked Janet. "I didn't know you'd made any, Aunt Sallie."

"It isn't exactly ice-cream," answered Uncle Toby's housekeeper. "It's a sort of snow-cream I made, but maybe you children will like it."

"Sure we will!" cried the boys.

"Will you have it now, or the plum pudding?" Aunt Sallie wanted to know.

"Oh, is there plum pudding, too?" Janet asked, in surprise.

"Yes," nodded Aunt Sallie. "Nice, hot plum pudding!"

"Let's have the pudding last," suggested Lola. "The snow-cream will make us cold and the plum pudding will make us warm again."

"A good idea," said Uncle Toby, with a laugh. "I hope none of the children gets ill," he thought to himself. "Their folks will say I gave them too much Thanksgiving. But they look all right now," he added, as he scanned the happy faces.

Aunt Sallie served the snow-cream. It was rather like a frozen pudding, being made of clean snow beaten up with milk, eggs, sugar, and flavoring extract.

The children made away with this, and then Aunt Sallie went to the kitchen to get the hot plum pudding. She was gone a few minutes when she came hurrying back into the dining room, a strange look on her face.

"It's gone!" she cried to Uncle Toby.

"What?" he asked.

"The plum pudding! Some one has taken it!"

CHAPTER XIX

SKYROCKET IS GONE

Uncle Toby first looked around the table at the double row of faces of the children. All showed as much surprise as had Aunt Sallie when she had come in with the news about the pudding being gone. At first Uncle Toby had an idea that one of the boys had taken the dessert for a joke, hiding it away in some nook. But one look at the faces of Tom, Ted, and Harry showed Uncle Toby that this had not happened.

"Where did you put the pudding, Aunt Sallie?" Uncle Toby wanted to know.

"Right inside the kitchen pantry, on the back shelf near the window."

"Was the window open, Aunt Sallie?"

"Just a little crack, yes, Uncle Toby. I opened it when I set the pudding near it so it would cool a little before the children ate it."

"That accounts for it then!" exclaimed Mr. Bardeen. "Skyrocket reached in through the open window and took the pudding!"

There was a gasp of surprise from the children at this, and Ted exclaimed:

"Oh, it couldn't have been our dog, Uncle Toby! He's been right here in the room all the while."

"Yes, that's so," added Aunt Sallie. "And, anyhow, the window wasn't open wide enough for Skyrocket to get his head in. He couldn't take the pudding out in his paw as your monkey could do."

"Maybe not," agreed Uncle Toby. "Anyhow, I'm glad to know it wasn't Skyrocket, for I like that dog. But some one must have taken the pudding, Aunt Sallie. Unless it slipped out of the window itself, and went off on the toboggan!"

The children laughed at this idea, but Aunt Sallie took it seriously, for she said:

"Oh, it couldn't do that, Uncle Toby. I mean it couldn't slip out of the window," she added, as the Curlytops laughed again. "I had it covered with a tin pan, and that's on the shelf, but the pudding is gone from under it."

"This is getting mysterious," said Uncle Toby. "We must take a look and see about it."

"I'm so sorry, for I wanted the children to have some of my plum pudding," went on Aunt Sallie.

"Oh, don't worry about it," said Lola. "We had plenty to eat."

"Too much, I'm afraid," chuckled Uncle Toby. "Maybe it's just as well the pudding is missing. The children will sleep better without it, Aunt Sallie."

"Oh, 'tisn't so much the *pudding* that I am worried about," went on the kindly housekeeper, in a whisper. "It is that some one may be sneaking around here taking things."

"Do you think that happened?" asked Uncle Toby. The children had run into the kitchen to look at the window through which the pudding had so mysteriously disappeared, and Uncle Toby and Aunt Sallie could speak freely.

"Yes, Uncle Toby, I think that is what happened," said the old lady. "Some tramp, or somebody, must have been sneaking around your cabin. They looked in the window, saw my pudding, and took it while we were all in the dining room. 'Tisn't so much that I mind the pudding; that is, if it was taken by some one really hungry. For this is Thanksgiving, and I wouldn't want any one to go hungry. But if they had knocked at the door and asked for something to eat I'd have given it to them, and then the pudding would be safe. What are we going to do?"

"I don't know," answered Uncle Toby, as he and Aunt Sallie followed the children. "We never had any tramps in these woods. Maybe it's that queer man we saw over in Newt Baker's old shack. He may be a hungry tramp."

"Well, something ought to be done about it," declared Aunt Sallie. "I won't feel safe with such people roaming the woods."

"Maybe when I look in the snow under the window I'll see the paw marks of a bear," suggested Uncle Toby.

"What would that mean?" asked Aunt Sallie, rather startled.

"It would mean that a bear came up, put his paws in through the window, knocked the pan cover off and took the pudding," was the answer.

"Well, I'm not so much afraid of bears as I am of tramps," said Aunt Sallie, with a smile. "I almost wish it was a bear!"

But it was not. In the light covering of newly fallen snow under the pantry window, through which the pudding had been taken, were the marks of a man's feet. Big feet they were, with heavy shoes, for the prints of the hob nails could be seen in the snow.

Uncle Toby looked at the marks for several minutes. He and Aunt Sallie and the children could see where the man, whoever he was, had come out of the woods, walked up to the open window, and, after standing about and tramping to and fro, had marched back to the woods again.

"It looks as if he came here, looked in, saw the pudding, and started away without taking it," said Uncle Toby, as he looked closely at the big footprints in the snow. "Then he turned back, because he was so hungry he just couldn't leave that pudding there in plain sight, I suppose. He took it and went back to the woods with it to eat it."

"Who was he?" asked Tom.

"That I don't know," Uncle Toby replied. "He must be a stranger around here, for anybody else would ask for something to eat if he were hungry. And most of the folks around here are well enough off to get their own Thanksgiving dinner. They don't have to take other folks' pudding."

"That's so," said Aunt Sallie. "I wish it hadn't happened, even though I don't mind a poor hungry man having my nice pudding."

"Is your dog a bloodhound?" asked Harry of Ted, as the boys remained looking at the footprints in the snow, after the girls had gone back into the house with Aunt Sallie.

"Oh, no, Skyrocket isn't a bloodhound," answered Ted. "Why?"

"Well, I thought maybe if he was he could smell at these marks in the snow and then track the man to where he was and we could get back the pudding," Harry went on.

"Guess there wouldn't be much of the pudding left," said Tom, with a laugh.

"No," agreed Ted. "Anyhow, Skyrocket isn't a bloodhound, and I don't believe he'd know how to track a man down."

And evidently Skyrocket didn't take much interest in the strange footprints in the snow, for, after sniffing them once or twice, he raced away to chase a snowbird which flew down to get the crumbs Aunt Sallie scattered from the dinner table. Of course Skyrocket couldn't catch or harm the snowbird, and he knew it, but he loved to race about and bark.

"No use trying to get him to follow a trail," said Tom. "He's too crazy! A good dog, but too crazy!"

"That's right!" assented Ted.

Uncle Toby, having listened to the talk of the boys, went back into the cabin, and soon came out with his heavy overcoat and cap on.

"Where are you going?" asked Ted.

"Oh, just down to the village. You boys stay here and look after things until I get back," was the answer.

The boys watched Uncle Toby strike into the path and then Tom exclaimed:

"I know where he's going!"

"Where?" asked Ted.

"He's either going to trail that man by his footprints—the man who took the pudding," declared Tom, "or else he's going to get a constable, or somebody like a policeman."

"Maybe he's gone to get a bloodhound if your dog isn't any good for smelling out people," suggested Harry. All the boys were gleefully excited over what might happen.

"I wish he'd let us go with him," sighed Ted. But he did not think it wise to ask, and Uncle Toby went off by himself.

The remainder of Thanksgiving was passed by the Curlytops and their playmates having holiday fun. They played out in the snow, spent some time in the snow house, and coasted on the toboggan.

Uncle Toby came back before dusk, but where he had been and what he had done or found out, he did not disclose to Aunt Sallie or the children.

"Will you lock up well to-night, Uncle Toby?" asked Aunt Sallie, when the bedtime hour approached. She asked this out of the hearing of the children.

"Of course I'll lock up well. I do every night," Uncle Toby replied, with a laugh. "Are you afraid that bear who took the pudding will try to get in?"

"Maybe," answered Aunt Sallie. "Anyhow, please lock all the doors and windows."

"I will," said Uncle Toby. "But I guess Skyrocket will be a good watchdog during the night. We don't need to worry."

The children did not worry, at all events. They did not seem to miss the plum pudding, and after a light supper, on account of the heavy dinner they had eaten, and having played some games in the cabin, they went to sleep.

Uncle Toby locked up well, and left Skyrocket in the kitchen for the night.

"If any bears come in or any tramps try to take any more of Aunt Sallie's good things, you grab 'em and hold 'em, Sky!" commanded Uncle Toby.

The dog barked once, as if to say he would.

The night appeared to pass quietly, though once Uncle Toby thought he heard Skyrocket barking in the kitchen. Getting out of his bed, Uncle Toby called:

"Who's in the kitchen? Is everything all right?"

There was no answer, not even a bark from the dog, and Uncle Toby thought he had been mistaken about hearing a noise.

"And I guess Skyrocket is asleep," he added.

In the morning Tom and Ted came down earlier than any of the others, for they had an idea that they could build a little house of pieces of carpet on the toboggan and coast while inside it. They wanted to try out this idea before Uncle Toby should say it was too risky.

"Here, Sky! Sky!" called Ted, as he walked toward the kitchen.

There was no joyous, answering bark, and when the door was pushed open no dog ran to greet his young master.

Skyrocket was gone!

CHAPTER XX

TROUBLE IS MISSING

Harry came into the kitchen to join his chums, and when he heard that Skyrocket was gone he and the other two boys made such a noise calling and whistling for the missing dog that Uncle Toby asked:

"What's the matter out there?"

"Skyrocket's gone!" explained Ted.

"Well, that's all right," said Uncle Toby. "I suppose he went out early to get up an appetite for breakfast."

"But how could he get out, Uncle Toby?" asked Ted, as Mr. Bardeen came into the kitchen where the dog had been put for the night. "How could he get out? There isn't a door or window open, and he hasn't jumped through any of the window glass, as he did once to get to me when he was shut up by mistake."

"Hum!" murmured Uncle Toby, thoughtfully. "Are you sure he's gone, Ted?"

"Well, he isn't around and he doesn't come when I call him," the boy answered. "He must be gone."

Jan and the other girls now came into the kitchen, and soon Aunt Sallie had Trouble dressed, so the whole family was up. That is all but Skyrocket, and he surely was one of the family.

"What's the matter?" asked Jan, for she knew that there was something wrong. And when Ted told her about Skyrocket being gone, tears came into Jan's eyes. Seeing this, Uncle Toby knew what he had to do to keep the children contented and happy while on their holiday stay with him at Crystal Lake.

"Look here, boys and girls," he said, "Skyrocket isn't lost. He has just run out somewhere. He'll be back soon. Don't feel too bad about him. It isn't the first time he has run away, is it, Ted?"

"No, Uncle Toby. But how did he get out to run away? That's what I want to know. There isn't a door or window open. The cabin was shut tight last night after Skyrocket was in."

"That's what we think," said Uncle Toby. "But some door or window may have been left open by mistake, and Skyrocket may have got out that way and be roaming in the woods, having a good time. Don't you often find, Aunt Sallie," asked Uncle Toby, "that you forget to shut a door or window, and later in the night get up to close it?"

As Mr. Bardeen asked this question of his housekeeper he winked one eye at her—an eye the children could not see. Uncle Toby wanted Aunt Sallie to say "yes" to his question, and she, knowing the little trick he was trying to play, did as he wanted her to.

"There, you are!" exclaimed Uncle Toby to the children. "Aunt Sallie or I may have left a door or window open, after you young folks went to bed, and Sky may have gotten out that way. Then we might have closed it, locking him out."

"Oh, do you think it could have happened that way?" asked Ted.

"Of course it could!" replied Uncle Toby, but he did not really say that it had happened like that. In fact Uncle Toby knew it had not happened this way. He felt pretty sure that some one had come in the night and stolen Skyrocket away, but he did not want to tell the Curlytops this for fear of making them afraid.

"Well, if Skyrocket has just run away he'll run back again," said Ted.

"Yes, he will, for he's done it before," added Janet.

Then the children felt better, and sat down to breakfast. But when Uncle Toby had a chance to speak quietly to Aunt Sallie he said:

"Don't say anything to the children, but I think some tramp—maybe the same one who took your plum pudding—came in the night and stole Skyrocket."

"But why would a tramp want Skyrocket?" asked Aunt Sallie.

"Perhaps he thought we would pay money to get the dog back—as I will do if he doesn't come back himself," said Uncle Toby. "You can't tell what a tramp would do. Anyhow, I know we didn't leave any doors or windows open. I just said that to quiet the children. I feel sure Skyrocket has been stolen by a tramp."

"What are you going to do about it, Uncle Toby?"

"I'm going to get Jim Nelson and some of the lumbermen around here and have a look around. For one place, we'll go to that old cabin of Newt Baker's, which we saw the man running away from that day. Maybe he's the tramp who took Skyrocket and also your plum pudding."

"Dear me!" exclaimed Aunt Sallie, with a frightened look over her shoulder.

"Don't be afraid!" laughed Uncle Toby. "Nothing will happen. But I don't want the children's fun spoiled. So let them think Skyrocket just wandered away and will come back again."

But Skyrocket did not come back that day nor the next nor the next. Back home in Cresco he had often stayed away a week at a time, Jan said, so after she and her brother had gotten used to the idea that the dog was off on one of his wandering trips, they no longer worried.

Uncle Toby got some of the lumbermen and went to the cabin, but though they found the footprints of men and dogs in the snow, no one was now in the old shack, and there was no way of telling whether the dog's footprints were those of Skyrocket.

"Well, I guess that tramp cleared out," said Uncle Toby to Aunt Sallie. "And he may have taken Skyrocket with him. But don't say anything to the Curlytops. Christmas is coming, and we want them to have a good time. And Skyrocket may come back."

But the dog did not. Two weeks went by and he had not returned. By this time Ted and Janet had rather gotten accustomed to missing him, and though they felt very sorry, they were having so much fun that they thought of little else. For surely there were good times at Uncle Toby's!

The plan of the boys to put up a little carpet house on the big toboggan coaster did not work. They tried it, without telling Uncle Toby anything about it, and this is what happened.

First Tom, Ted, and Harry fastened some beanpoles upright on the toboggan. They tied them tightly with cords so they were fairly solid. In the barn they found some pieces of carpet and a few old feed bags, left from the time that Uncle Toby kept a horse out at Crystal Lake, and by tying these bags together, after ripping them open, they made a large piece of cloth, big enough for a tent. This they fastened on the beanpoles that were tied to the toboggan, also using some carpet strips.

"Now we've got a regular little house on it, and we can sit inside and coast downhill and be nice and warm!" exclaimed Ted.

That was his idea and that of the other boys. Three of them could get inside the toboggan-tent at a time, and the rear lad could stick his foot out through a hole in the bag covering a steer.

Without telling Uncle Toby anything about it, and saying nothing to the girls, the boys drew this new invention of theirs out on the coasting hill one morning. Tom and Harry took their places toward the front of the toboggan, inside the tent. There was a hole in the bagging so they could look out. Ted sat behind to steer.

"All ready?" he asked his chums.

"Let her go!" cried Tom.

Ted pushed off, and for a little way the toboggan went down the hill all right. The boys were laughing and shouting, for it was fun to coast inside a tent that kept off the cold wind.

"It's like riding in a closed auto!" yelled Tom.

But just then something happened. The toboggan struck a lump of ice on the hill, slued around, though Ted did his best to steer it, and began going sideways.

Just then the three girls, with Trouble, came out to see what the boys were doing, and seeing the strange tent-covered toboggan going downhill sideways Janet, Lola, and Mary, all three, screamed, while Trouble yelled in delight, as he always did at anything new or strange.

Ted declared afterward that the girls' screams made him steer crooked, but in the girls' opinion the toboggan would have upset anyhow. And that's what it did.

Over it turned, when half way down the hill. The bean poles snapped and broke, and a moment later the boys were tangled up in the pieces of carpet and bagging, rolling off the toboggan which coasted the rest of the way downhill by itself, and probably it was very glad to be rid of the tent-house.

"Oh, are you hurt?" cried Jan, as she saw the tangled mass of boys.

"I'll call Uncle Toby!" exclaimed Lola.

"Oh, what a dreadful accident!" wailed Mary.

But an instant later the boys jumped up, laughing, not in the least hurt, though they were disappointed because their invention did not work.

"Don't try any more tricks like that," said Uncle Toby, when he heard what had happened. "The next time some of you may be hurt."

The boys promised to obey, and they didn't do any thing just like that again, but they did other things almost as risky. However, no one was hurt, and they certainly had lots of fun at Uncle Toby's.

There was so much to do that they almost forgot about the lost Skyrocket, though every now and then Ted and his chums would go off in the woods, whistling and calling. But the dog did not come back.

As the snow did not melt away, Uncle Toby, with the help of some of his men friends at the camp, cleared a place on the frozen lake where the children could skate. And with this fun, with coasting, making snowmen, another snow house, having snowball battles, the children passed many days most happily.

Christmas was coming. The Curlytops and their playmates now began counting the days until this grand holiday should arrive. Trouble, with the help of Janet, had written his letter to Santa Claus, and the other children had told each other (so Aunt Sallie and Uncle Toby could hear) the things they wished St. Nicholas to bring them.

One morning Uncle Toby brought the big automobile around to the door of the cabin. It was two days before Christmas, and everything had been prepared for a jolly good time at the cabin. A big green tree had been cut in the woods, and set up in one of the rooms. There it was to be trimmed and made ready for the presents to be put under it.

"Come, children, we're going to the village to get the mail and some other things," called Uncle Toby to the Curlytops and their friends. "Pile in, and we'll all go to the village. I wouldn't be surprised but what there would be some letters for all of you," he said, with a twinkle in his eyes, as if he knew what was going to happen.

"Oh, maybe daddy and mother will be here for Christmas!" cried Ted and Janet.

"And maybe my father and mother will come," added Lola, though she did not have much hope of this.

"If I could get a letter that my mother was all well again, that would be the best Christmas present I could have," sighed Mary.

"Maybe you will get such a letter," said Uncle Toby.

Perhaps he knew what was going to happen.

Aunt Sallie said she would not make the trip to the village in the automobile, as she had work to do at the bungalow. So Uncle Toby, the Curlytops and their playmates—alas, not with Skyrocket this time—started off. The snow seemed to be coming down thicker and faster, but this only made the children more joyful, for they loved snow at Christmas, as what youngster does not?

The post-office was reached, and Uncle Toby went in for the mail. He came out with both hands full. There was a letter for Mary and Harry, one for Ted and Janet and one for Tom and Lola, and then there were separate letters for each boy and girl from some of the friends they had left behind. There was even a postal for Trouble.

"Oh, such good news!" cried Ted, when he and Janet had read their letter. "Daddy and Mother are coming here to spend Christmas with us!"

"Did your father say anything about the money he was afraid of losing?" asked Uncle Toby.

"No," answered Ted. "But I hope he doesn't lose it."

"We have good news, like yours!" Lola said to Janet. "Our daddy and mother are coming here also for Christmas. You invited them, didn't you, Uncle Toby?" she asked.

"Why, yes, I believe I did," chuckled the jolly old gentleman. "But have you good news, too?" he asked Harry and Mary.

"Yes," they answered with happy tears in their eyes. "Our mother is well again, and she is coming up here for Christmas. Oh, how happy we are!"

"Everybody's happy!" sang Trouble. "Everybody's happy, an' Santa C'aus is comin'!"

"That's right!" laughed Janet, hugging him.

They little knew how close unhappiness was following happiness.

After the letters had been read again Uncle Toby drove the automobile down the village street to the store to get some things Aunt Sallie wanted for the Christmas dinner. As the children each had some spending money they were allowed to get out and wander through a general store next to the grocery. There was a "five and ten cent" department in the variety "Emporium" as it was called, and the children had fun there, picking out inexpensive presents as surprises one for the other.

It was not until, bubbling over with joy and happiness, they had again gotten back in the automobile that Trouble was missed.

"Oh, where is your little brother?" exclaimed Lola.

"Why, I thought you had him!" said Janet.

"And I thought you did. We must have left him back in the store. Let's look!"

But Trouble was not there! He was missing!

CHAPTER XXI

TROUBLE AND SKYROCKET

You can imagine there was much excitement and some very frightened feelings in the hearts of all the children when the clerks in the store where the five and ten cent Christmas presents had been bought said Trouble was not there.

"But where can he be?" asked Janet, hardly able to keep back the tears.

"Perhaps he went out and walked back to the store where Uncle Toby is buying his things," suggested Lola. "Let's look there."

"I guess that's where he is all right," said Teddy.

But Trouble was not in the grocery store, and Uncle Toby, who had finished his shopping, was as much surprised and alarmed as were the children when told what had happened.

"I guess the little tyke may have walked out by himself and gotten into the auto," said Uncle Toby.

But Trouble was not in the big closed automobile. And then a frantic search began. People in the stores where Uncle Toby and the children had been lent their aid, and when after fifteen minutes it was sure that the little boy was not in the neighborhood, the constable was called on and the search made up and down the street.

"Well, we'll find him, of course," said Uncle Toby, speaking more hopefully than he really felt. "What happened, I suppose, is that he wandered out of the store, to find me, maybe, and he got in the wrong place. We'll look in every building along Main Street."

This was done, and the houses on side streets were visited, too, but without effect. Trouble seemed to have vanished completely and mysteriously.

By this time Janet was crying, as were the other girls, and the boys tried not to let the tears in their eyes be seen.

"Where can he be?" asked the Curlytops over and over again, when each store had been searched twice.

"I'll tell you what I think happened," said Uncle Toby. "Trouble wandered away from you, while you were buying your Christmas presents. He wandered out into the street and got confused. Maybe he started crying in the street, and some farmer and his wife, in their sled, may have taken him in to comfort him."

"But what would they do with him?" asked Ted.

"Some farmer and his wife picked Trouble up off the street and took him home with them," repeated Mr. Bardeen, as if he knew this was so. And he really believed it.

"Why would they do that?" asked Jan, with trembling lips.

"They may have thought Trouble was the child of some neighbor whom they knew, and they planned to take him home. Depend on it—that's what happened!"

"But how will we get Trouble back?" asked Ted.

"Why, the farmer, whoever he is, will find out his mistake, and he'll bring the little fellow back to town again," was the answer. "That's what will happen. But I'll get as many men as I can, and with the constable we'll inquire of all the farmers around here. In that way we'll get Trouble back quicker."

There were willing searchers, and soon the country around Crystal Lake was being searched by men and women in automobiles and sleds who inquired at each farmhouse for a little boy taken away by mistake.

But as night came and no Trouble had been found, the Curlytops and their playmates began to feel very sad indeed.

Uncle Toby decided to take the children home and leave them with Aunt Sallie in the cabin, while he kept on with the search.

"Trouble missing and Skyrocket gone!" thought Uncle Toby to himself, as he drove back in the automobile. "This will be a sad Christmas, when I meant it to be such a happy one."

But it would not be Christmas for two days, and much might happen in that time.

It was nearly dusk when the big automobile drew near the old deserted cabin of Newt Baker, from which the strange man had once been seen running away. Looking from the window on his side, Ted peered at the old shack, and as he did so he uttered a cry of surprise and wonder.

"What is it?" asked Uncle Toby, quickly bringing the machine to a stop, for he thought some one had opened a door and fallen out.

"It's Trouble! I saw him at the window just now! In there!" and Ted pointed to the old cabin.

"Trouble in there? It can't be!" said Uncle Toby.

But just then Janet set up a cry.

"Yes, he is, Uncle Toby! I saw him!"

Mr. Bardeen lost little time in jumping from the automobile. Followed by the children, he ran to the door of the cabin, and as he opened it he heard the barking of a dog mingled with the crying voice of Trouble. An instant later Skyrocket rushed out to greet his friends, and then Trouble came from an inner room, toddling into the arms of Janet.

"Oh, William! how did you ever get here?" cried Lola.

"And Skyrocket, too! Look! Here's our dog!" shouted Ted.

With the high voices of the children, the barking of Skyrocket, and the crying of Trouble, there was so much noise that no one heard footsteps coming from the room out of which the missing boy had rushed until suddenly a strange man stood on the threshold.

"Look!" cried Tom, glancing up at this man. "There's the tramp!"

And they all saw the same stranger who had rushed away from the cottage the time Uncle Toby went to the well to get water for the automobile radiator.

"What are you doing here?" asked Uncle Toby in a stern voice. "And did you try to kidnap him?" Mr. Bardeen pointed to little William, who was sobbing in Janet's arms. And as he saw this and thought what a lot of trouble seemed to have been caused by this man, Uncle Toby started toward him as if in anger.

"Don't hit me!" pleaded the man. "I'm in trouble! I've had a lot of trouble. I was in the war—and—but that was long ago—and—"

His voice was very faint, and as Uncle Toby walked toward him the man tried to run back into the room. But his foot slipped and he fell, striking his head heavily on the floor. Then he rolled over and lay very quiet.

"He's fainted, I guess," said Tom.

"Looks so," agreed Uncle Toby. "Well, we've found Trouble, anyhow. That's the big thing. I don't know how this man got him or what he intended to do with him. But I'm going to tell the police. I guess he'd better have a doctor, too," he added. "He's cut his head in his fall. Ted, you and Tom go to the next house," he went on. "There's a telephone there. Tell Mr. Hick to call up the police, let them know we have found the missing boy and have them send out a doctor. It's a long walk to Mr. Hick's place, but I guess you won't be afraid. Then come back here. I don't want to leave this man alone, as I'd have to do if we all went away in the auto."

"We'll go to the telephone," said Tom and Ted, and Harry went with them.

As soon as the boys started tramping through the gathering dusk to Mr. Hick's house, Janet quieted Trouble and got Skyrocket to stop barking. This last was hard because the dog was so overjoyed at being with his friends again. There was a broken rope around his neck, showing that he had been kept tied up since he had been taken away. But he seemed to have been well treated and fed.

"Can Trouble tell us what happened and how this man got him?" asked Uncle Toby of Janet, who was holding her little brother. The "tramp," as he was called, still lay where he had fallen in a faint.

Janet understood Trouble's baby talk better than any one else, and she soon had his story out of him. He had wandered out of the store, it seemed, and on the sidewalk in front had been spoken to by the man who had brought him to the lonely cabin. The tramp and Trouble rode out to the cabin in a farmer's sled, so the little boy said.

"I can understand how that might happen," said Uncle Toby. "Some farmer would be glad to give the man and Trouble a ride out into the country. And it might have been some farmer from a distance, who didn't know that no one lived here. Such a farmer wouldn't be surprised at Trouble and the man getting out here at the lonely cabin. Well, things are coming out all right, and maybe this tramp didn't intend to do anything mean. We'll have to wait until he gets better so he can tell us what happened."

The stranger was still lying very quiet on the floor of the lonely cabin. It was a long time before the three boys came back, but soon after them the constable and the doctor arrived. The doctor said the man was not badly hurt, but should have good care. And as it was thought he might have tried to kidnap Trouble he was put under arrest.

Of course the man himself did not know this, for he was still in a faint. The doctor said the blow on his head caused this. But he was taken away by the constable and the doctor to the doctor's own home, where he could be well cared for until he was well enough to be put in jail, for he was under arrest for having carried off Trouble.

Then the Curlytops and their playmates went on to Uncle Toby's cabin, a happy jolly crowd, now that all worry was removed. They had William with them, and also Skyrocket.

"But I wonder how that tramp got my dog?" mused Ted.

"He might have found him wandering in the woods," said Uncle Toby. But he did not really believe this. There was something queer about that tramp.

CHAPTER XXII

A HAPPY REUNION

Such joyous times as there were next day! It was the day before Christmas, and, as every one knows, it is the jolliest time in the year, with one exception. That exception is Christmas itself.

"When are we going to the station to meet the folks?" asked the Curlytops and their playmates, over and over again. For Mr. and Mrs. Martin, Mr. and Mrs. Taylor, and the mother of Harry and Mary, now out of the hospital, were to come on the same train, to spend the Christmas holidays at Uncle Toby's.

"Oh, we'll go soon now," said Mr. Bardeen, and the children could hardly wait. Uncle Toby had arranged for an extra automobile to bring the grown folks from the station to his cabin, as the Bardeen car would be well filled.

After what seemed many hours, though it was really not more than a wait of thirty minutes at the station, the toot of a whistle was heard around a curve in the track.

"Here comes the train!" cried Ted.

"Oh, what a lovely Christmas this is going to be!" sighed Janet.

Out of the car came the mother and father of the Curlytops, then the mother and father of Tom and Lola, and then, more slowly, Mrs. Benton.

"Oh, we're so glad to see you!" cried the Curlytops and their playmates, each to the proper parents. There was hugging and kissing, and in excited tones the story of the missing boy and dog was quickly told.

"It is very good of you, Mr. Bardeen, to ask me out here," said Mrs. Benton. "I feel sure I shall grow well and strong now, and I can look after my two children."

"That's all right, Susan!" was the hearty answer. "I'm glad to have you and the children. We're going to have a jolly Christmas."

And indeed it seemed so, for Mr. and Mrs. Martin found a chance to tell Ted and Janet that it was all right about the money—that Mr. Martin was not going to lose it after all. His trip had saved it for him.

As the automobiles were about to start off, the constable came up to Uncle Toby and said:

"That strange man—the one who fell and hurt himself at the cabin when you found the kidnapped boy—wants to see you, Mr. Bardeen."

"Wants to see me?" asked Uncle Toby, in surprise.

"Yes. It seems he is much better now, and is in his right mind."

"Was he out of his mind before?" asked Uncle Toby, while the others listened eagerly.

"Yes, he was most of the time, though not always. He's a soldier, it seems, or was. He fought in the big war and was hurt or gassed, or something, and lost his mind. He really doesn't know what happened to him, except that he ran away from different hospitals, got to this country somehow, and has been wandering around ever since, living as best he could. But he's all right now. The doctor said that fall he had did something to his head and gave him back his right senses, so he's all right now, and he's asking for you."

"What's his name, and why does he want to see me?" asked Uncle Toby.

"He says he wants to explain that he didn't try to kidnap the little boy," the constable went on. "And he didn't steal the dog, either. The dog came to the cabin, made friends with him, and the man kept him. Though maybe the dog would have gone to you if he hadn't been tied up. But the man's very anxious to see you and explain all this. I said I'd go get you. I went out to your cabin, and a lady there said you'd come here to the station, so I hurried back, and here I am. Could you come and see that man for a few minutes?"

"Why, I suppose I could, yes," answered Uncle Toby. "But who is he, anyhow? You say he was a soldier in the big war?"

"Yes. And he says his name is Frank Benton. He—"

But there was an excited cry from the mother of Mary and Harry.

"Frank Benton!" she exclaimed. "Why, that was my husband's name! My husband fought in the war! We thought he was killed, but we never could be sure of it, as no record was found. Oh, if this should be your missing father, children!" and with tears in her eyes she looked at her boy and girl.

"We'll soon find out!" cried Uncle Toby.

"To the doctor's! First house around that corner," directed the constable.

Trembling with eagerness and hope, Mrs. Benton, with Harry and Mary, went into the room where the injured man lay in a white bed. He was much better now, and the constable did not go along, since he was not to be arrested, as what he had done had been when he was out of his head through a war injury.

"Frank!" cried Mrs. Benton, as soon as she caught sight of the man.

"Susan!" he murmured, holding out his arms. And then such a happy reunion as there was. "My, how big the children have become!" exclaimed Mr. Benton, through his glad tears. "To think I saw them in the room with the Curlytops and didn't know them."

"And they didn't know you," said his wife. "But now we have each other! Oh, how happy I am. This will be the best Christmas in all the world!"

And it was—for every one at Uncle Toby's cabin.

There is not much more to tell. The mystery was all cleared up. Mr. Benton had been wounded in the war, an injury to his brain making him out of his head, though not dangerously so. He wandered away, escaping from one hospital after another under the mistaken notion that the doctors and nurses were trying to harm him.

In his wanderings he finally reached the neighborhood of Crystal Lake. He found the old deserted cabin and made his home there, living on what he could pick up or take from the farmhouses. Thus the rumor of tramps and burglars was talked of at the lake. Poor Mr. Benton was so timid that he ran away when Uncle Toby came to draw water.

It was Mr. Benton who took Aunt Sallie's plum pudding from the pantry, though he did not know he was stealing. And it was he who looked in the window, thus frightening Janet. And, as he said, he had found Skyrocket wandering in the woods. There was a loose board on one side of the cabin, a board Uncle Toby had forgotten about, and Skyrocket got out through that hole the night he disappeared. After getting him to the lonely cabin Mr. Benton became so fond of the dog that he tied him up. Though Skyrocket might have remained of his own accord, for he had made friends with the wounded soldier.

It was while strolling about the streets of the village that the father of Mary and Harry saw Trouble wandering out of the five and ten cent store. Always fond of children, Mr. Benton made friends with William, and Trouble took a liking to the strange man.

Then, somehow or other, the idea of taking Trouble to the lonely cabin came into the head of the man, and he got a ride out in the sled of a strange farmer. But once in the deserted shack Trouble became frightened and began to cry. Mr. Benton did not know what to do, his head was troubling him, and he realized dimly that he might get into difficulties with the police. He left Trouble in a room, trying to think what was best to do to get the little boy back to his friends, and then Uncle Toby came along.

After that things happened quickly. Mr. Benton slipped and fell, and the blow on his head did what the doctors and nurses could not seem to do for him. It brought him back to his right mind.

"And we'll soon have you out at my cabin, spending Christmas with the Curlytops!" said Uncle Toby, when everything had been explained.

"Oh, what a happy time it will be!" said Mr. Benton.

That night he was taken out to the cabin, and there was reunited with his little family. And such a gladsome, happy, and thankful Christmas eve was never known before!

It seemed that the children never would go to bed, but at last they quieted down and then—well, what always happens on Christmas eve took place after that.

The Christmas tree was wondrously trimmed, empty stockings began to swell out and there was even one for Skyrocket which was laden to overflowing with dog biscuit.

The sun shone bright on the snow around Crystal Lake.

"Merry Christmas!" cried the Curlytops, as they rushed to see what Santa Claus had left for them.

"Merry Christmas!" echoed their playmates.

"The happiest Christmas in all the world!" said Harry and Mary. For they had found their father, long lost to them.

"I 'ikes Ch'is'mus," murmured Trouble, his mouth full of candy. "I 'ikes Ch'is'mus an' Unk Toby an' everybody! I 'ike 'oo!" he said to Mr. Benton.

"And I like you," said the father of Mary and Harry. "Only for you and Uncle Toby I might not be here, happy with my family. Merry Christmas to everybody!"

And so, with the gladsome echoes of "Merry Christmas" filling the air, we will say good-bye to the Curlytops.

End of the book.

www.ingramcontent.com/pod-product-compliance
Lightning Source LLC
Chambersburg PA
CBHW070702290526
45790CB00001B/408